Aunt Sadie's Letters of Hope & Healing

Shari Lyn Anderson

Copyright © 2021 Shari Lyn Anderson.

All rights reserved. This book is protected by copyright. No part of this book may be reproduced or transmitted in any form or by any means, including as photocopies or scanned-in or other electronic copies, or utilized by any information storage and retrieval system without written permission from the copyright owner.

Printed in the United States of America.

Cover design by 100Covers
Interior design by FormattedBooks

Dedicated to the loving memory
of my mother, Rhoda Winters,
and my Great-Aunt Sadie Kleinberg

ACKNOWLEDGEMENTS

It has been said it takes a village, no truer words can be said for making this project possible. It is my pleasure to thank the many people who have assisted me in this endeavor.

When I decided to take on this endeavor, I was unaware of what was involved in publishing a book. I was naïve to the process and with the support of family and friends, they made it possible for me to share my mother's journey.

First, I would like to thank my mother of blessed memory, who saved all of these letters from her aunt, making this book a possibility. To my great-aunt for her love and devotion to my mother.

Thank you to my supportive husband, Chuck, whose encouragement, emotional support, and advocacy was unwavering. To my children, Jonathan, Jeffrey and Samantha who inspired and emboldened me to never give up and to accomplish my dreams. Thank you to some very special friends, Patty, Stephanie, and Tabitha, who championed me on and listened to my stories, whose enthusiasm kept me from being discouraged and continued to inspire me.

I would also like to thank my editor, Amanda Bidnall, and my publishing consultant, Bonni Goldberg whose patience, and guidance helped make my dream a reality.

INTRODUCTION

In the process of helping my mother clear out some things from her home, I came across a beautiful wicker basket. Inside was an abundance of letters: love letters from my father to my mother, Christmas and Valentine cards, telegrams and announcements. But what struck me the most were 101 letters written by my great-aunt to her ten-year-old niece—my mother—who was hospitalized with polio.

This is a collection of personal letters and poems written in wartime New York City. The author of the letters was my great-aunt, Sadie Kleinberg. The recipient was her niece—my mother—Rhoda Levine, who was stricken with polio in 1941. Rhoda, who lived in Brooklyn, New York, at the time, was ten years old and paralyzed from the waist down. My mother and her aunt had an extremely close bond, one that surpassed Rhoda's relationship with her own mother. My great-aunt passed on September 23, 1954, in Columbia, South Carolina, where she had finally settled with her husband. I was born eight months later and named after her.

According to census records, my mother's family immigrated to the United States from Russia, but they hailed from somewhere within the shifting borders of Poland. My great-grandfather immigrated in 1905, and my great-grandmother followed in 1906, bringing their three children. Per the census records, my great-aunt Sadie and my maternal grandmother were born in New York in 1907 and 1909 respectively. It appears that in the census year 1920, they were living in the New York City borough of Manhattan.

Twenty years later, a war was raging in Europe, and anti-Semitic feelings were at an all-time high. My great-aunt Sadie Kleinberg was in an untenable situation: out of work in a country where as many as eighty percent of Americans strongly opposed the admission of Jewish refugees. She felt that with a different name, more doors would be open to her. So she changed her name to Estelle King. This made a big impact, and she was able to find employment.

Almost all of the letters and poems in this book are signed "Aunt Sadie." However, all the envelopes bear the name Estelle King.

The United States government, during the late 1930s and early 1940s, strongly discouraged accepting refugees, as did many other governments worldwide. There were a few exceptions. The government in the Dominican Republic, for example, felt that Jews could improve the "racial inequalities" of their population. Bolivia, Switzerland, the Shanghai International Settlement, and the British Protectorate of Palestine also accepted Jewish refugees.

In the 1930s, President Hoover was adamantly opposed to bringing Jewish refugees to America, touting that the burden would increase unemployment. He stoked Americans' fears of a deepening depression.

During the Second World War, Americans' fear and hatred of those who were different from them was further complicated by their fear of refugees bringing communism, infiltrators and Nazi spies. There were many leaders who propagated this fear. Father Charles Coughlin preached anti-Semitism over the radio, claiming Jews were manipulating financial institutions and conspiring to control the world—a propaganda tool that is still widely accepted.

There were, however, those who disagreed with that ideology and worked tirelessly to turn that tide of thinking. In 1940, First Lady Eleanor Roosevelt supported the liberalization of immigration laws and worked behind the scenes to effect change. She also helped some individual refugees, specifically artists and intellectuals. The State Department saw things differently. They made it more difficult for Jewish refugees by making the visa application eight feet long and filling it with tiny print. It was the State Department that was responsible for turning away the infamous MS *St. Louis* in May 1939, compelling the ocean liner of Jewish refugees to return to Europe. Many former passengers ultimately perished in the Holocaust. Despite these efforts, approximately 200,000 Jews managed to reach American shores between 1933 and 1945.

Our country's attitudes today remind me of what was happening in the 1940s. There is great hate and distrust for anyone who is different from the so-called norm. It's sad to see that, in a lot of ways, little has changed in seventy-eight years.

My grandparents and extended family, including my great-aunt, wanted to be full-fledged Americans. They quickly assimilated to American culture and outwardly celebrated all the typical Christian holidays so as not to stand out and be different from other people. This did not, however, change who they were. My mother was not brought up in a religious household. She did not even know what the Jewish holidays were except that they existed through a special holiday meal. Unfortunately, my grandparents did not teach my mother about her Judaism. After my mother married and had children, she made sure her children went to Hebrew school and Sunday school to learn what she was never taught. She learned along with us, and although we were not religious, we certainly knew more about our Jewish heritage than she did when she was growing up. She made sure we were proud of who we were and knew the importance of being Jewish.

Rhoda was hospitalized at the beginning of November 1941. Her recollection of the exact date was unclear, but my great-aunt wrote her first letter to the hospital on November 13, 1941. When my mother was admitted, she was quarantined for as long as two weeks before being allowed to be in a ward with other children.

My aunt's last letter to my mother is dated March 31, 1942. My mother remembered coming home in time for the Passover holiday, which began on April 2 that year and ended on April 9. She told me the story about Palm Sunday, the week prior to Easter, which fell on April 5. The priest came in as he did every Sunday, and on this particular day he gave her palms. She politely accepted them, but she knew they weren't really meant for her. After the priest left, she gladly gave them to the little girl in the bed beside her. My mother recalls how happy it made that little girl's mom.

In 1941, visiting hours were kept to a minimum and strictly enforced. From what I can gather, my mother's visiting hours were on Wednesday and Sunday, and they lasted only one or two hours. I can't imagine how isolating and scary that must have been for a little girl.

Aunt Sadie's love for my mother was abounding and unending, and her pure affection for her niece oozes from every letter and poem. I started opening the letters in a most random fashion—they were just strewn about in the basket—and I was awestruck. Teary-eyed, I knew that these letters needed to be shared.

Sadie was a woman ahead of her time. Her love of the earth and humanity, her understanding of how precious both were, was, I believe, unusual for the times. My mother was extremely close with her. She loved her aunt dearly. I am blessed to be named after her. I wished I'd had the opportunity to meet such a talented and kind person, but she passed before I was born.

Aunt Sadie did eventually marry. He was an English professor, and when he received an opportunity to teach in England, they moved there for a period of time. They lived in Tunbridge Wells and traveled widely, taking in as much of the sights and culture as they could. No matter where my aunt was, she always kept in touch with my mother, filling her in on her exploits and travels. She spoke of Dublin, Belfast, Holyhead, Armagh, Liverpool and London. Sadie and her husband never had children of their own.

Reading her letters and poems over again, I began to understand how much they shaped my mother's character. Mom never had an ill word to say about anyone, and she always put her best face forward. She was trusting and treated everyone the same, no matter what they looked like, what they believed in, or even how they treated her. She saw the good in everyone. I sometimes found it hard to understand how she could be so forgiving when people treated her badly. From my perspective, she was always making excuses for them, but she saw it differently. She understood that they must not have meant it that way. I admired how she could rise above that and wished I could be more like her.

She told me many times that she didn't teach me or my brothers any lessons. She couldn't have been more wrong. My mother taught us how to treat other people with respect, how to act in kindness, and how to be loving despite how dismal things appeared. Her door was always open, and she welcomed anyone who walked through it, whether they were the repair man or cleaning lady. She always offered a drink or a bite to eat. It was all about what she could do for them. It almost seemed that she had a naivety about her, but I've come to learn it was just her nature to be compassionate, gracious, and hospitable. She was simply a very kind and understanding woman with an optimistic view of the world.

The following letters and poems mention several family members, so I will give a few introductions here.

>Larry: my mother Rhoda's brother and Sadie's nephew

>Sadie's siblings: Anna, Rhoda's mother, Laura (who died at a young age from diphtheria), Morris and Harry.

>Rhoda's cousins: Donald, Rina, Gladys, Sylvia, Alvin and Loretta (Loretta was believed to be so gorgeous that she was always referred to as "Gorgie").

I have preserved, as far as possible, the spelling, punctuation, and capitalization of the original letters in an effort to preserve the vibrancy of my great-aunt's language. Any necessary editorial changes are noted in the text.

November 13
1941

Dearest Rhoda,

Your mother speaks to me on the telephone almost every day, so I know exactly where you are and how you are. You may be sure I want to see you very much and so does everyone else want to see you. We will come just as soon as they will let us. This may take only about one more week. I am very glad that you will soon be with other children.

Now what do you think! I heard that you were not allowed to take anything out from the other place. Who cares! You are going to receive even nicer ones here, and more of them. I also heard that you could not take the book which Sylvia[*] sent you. This is the good part; I am getting you another book just like it so you can finish where you left off.

You know I like you to spread sunshine wherever you are, so, I am sending you this little card to remind you.

Love and kisses,

Aunt Sadie

---

[*] Sylvia was Sadie's niece and Rhoda's cousin.

November 15
1941

Dear little Sugar-Cookie,

Just as I told you, I went to Macy's on Saturday, and me oh my, did I get you a bunch of books! Of course, you will not begin to receive them for a few days yet, because first they will be sent to me, then I shall bring them to your mother, and then she will give them to you, one at a time.

Now I want to remind you once more. If you want anything special, whether it be a book or anything else, please be sure to ask your mother to tell me what it is, and then I will get it for you. I only hope you won't ask me to get you London Bridge!

By the way, I saw Sylvia on Friday night, and she told me that she also has a bunch of books which she is saving for you. She will give them to you soon.

Here is a poem I wrote especially for you:

> *There is a young lady named Rhoda*
> *Who loves to have ice cream and soda,*
> *But her aunt feeds her books and calls her "My Snooks,"*
> *Hurrah for the lady named Rhoda!*

Love and kisses from,

Aunt Sadie

November 16
1941

My dear little Sweetie-Pie,

> If children ate naught else but cake
> They'd always have a tummy ache
> But if they have sense in the head
> They'd also live on meat and bread

The same holds true for books and such. To read all kinds helps very much; read the funnies, and all about bunnies, the ways of the flowers and bees and honeys, of squirrels and trees and good mysteries. And why to cover your nose when you sneeze.

I could go on and write more funny little rhymes for you but I do not know whether you like these little poems, or not. Please tell your mother (of course I mean if you remember), and then she can tell me.

By that time the red roses will be old, I think I will get you some new ones. How would you like big chrysanthemums? That is a big word too.

Hugs and kisses,

Aunt Sadie

November 17
1941

My dear little Honeybunch,

Today your daddy spoke to me on the telephone, and it made me very happy to hear that you are getting better, a little bit better each day. He also told me why it is that you are getting better. It is because you are cooperating so beautifully with the doctors and the nurses. Keep it up, Rhoda dear.

Yesterday I went to the park with some of my friends and saw the cutest squirrels who stood on their hind legs and begged with their paws for nuts.

My friends walked in the park with me
When Miss Squirrel came running down a tree
"Look," said Frances, "how she stands on her legs,
and raises her paws, for nuts she begs"
We hadn't brought nuts to the park that day
So, sadly we had to turn her away
But later on, we came back, we brought Miss Squirrel some Cracker Jack.

Love from,

Aunt Sadie

November 18
1941

My dear little Ray of Sunshine,

How are you feeling today, are your words very kind, and the thoughts in your mind, helping you and the others to be gay?

How do you like the little girl who appears on the front of this letter? Shall we call her Mitzi or Bitzi, or perhaps Schnitzl? Tomorrow I will write you on paper that has a soldier boy standing on guard. Let us call him Fritzl. So, it will be Schnitzl and Fritzl following each other every day, playing hide and seek with each other.

Schnitzl and Fritzl, a girl and a boy
Which one is real, which is a toy?
Both are quite real, both are quite fine
They go one by one to my Ray of Sunshine!

With hundreds of hugs and kisses,

Aunt Sadie

November 19
1941

My dear little Sugar Plum,

> Here comes Fritzl, just as I said
> With a very silly looking hat stuck upon his head
> He's standing at attention, so he cannot bow to you
> He is very patriotic, dressed in red, white and blue
> He is looking for his Schnitzl, (they've been apart so long)
> Quick, tell him where she's hiding or he'll break his paper heart!

This afternoon your mother called me on the telephone, and I was very glad to hear that you are now among the other children. That is very good. I know you like to be near others, so I am sure you will enjoy it very much.

Uncle Harry and Uncle Morris, and Aunt Hattie* call me up nearly every day, so they know you are getting better and better. Isn't that wonderful?

On Saturday I may see your mother, and then I shall bring her all the books which I wrote about to you, so that she can begin to bring them to you beginning on Sunday.

If you have any special message for me, tell your mother on Sunday, or your daddy, and they can let me know.

I am glad that you liked and finished the "Mystery of the Hidden Staircase."

Love and kisses,

Aunt Sadie—I shall write again soon.

---

* Harry and Morris were Sadie's brothers. Hattie was Morris's wife.

November 21
1941

My dear little Goldilocks,

> *Raindrops are falling one by one*
> *Up goes my umbrella, and out goes the sun*
> *Who's afraid of raindrops, with umbrella held so high?*
> *Who's afraid of storm clouds, when the sun is in the sky?*
> *Have you an umbrella for a rainy day?*
> *What have you in your closet, to shoo the clouds away?*
> *I don't mind the raindrops, if they come once in a while*
> *Because they dry up mighty quick when I bring out my smile!*

And so, I hope you are having a wonderful time with Schnitzl and Fritzl. Next time I think I shall send you Miss Kitzl to work for the soldier boy and his lady. How would you like that? On Saturday I hope to see your mother and shall give you some loving messages through her.

Hugs oooo and kisses xxxx

With oodles of love,

From Aunt Sadie

November 22
1941

My dear little Buttercup,

Introducing the Kitzl

Schnitzl and Fritzl have so much to do, and no time in which to do it
Kitzl came along, and sang them a song, so, they hired her before she even knew it
She may look a little queer, but that's nothing my dear
What are looks when she makes them both happy?
She scrubs and she bakes she cooks and she sews
Yet, she often has time to powder her nose
That's because when she works, it is snappy!
When the day is done, they all join hands and
'round in a circle the three of them dance!

Saturday, I saw your mother for a little while, because I had to go home very soon, but I brought her the books. I want to tell you that mother showed me the very lovely letter which you wrote to your parents for Thanksgiving Day. It was simply delightful.

I was also happy to learn that you have begun to have regular classes with a teacher and will be able to keep up pretty well with your school work.

Continue to be pleasant to everybody, even though it is not always easy. In trying there is a great big victory.

With loads of love,

Aunt Sadie

November 23
1941

To my Sweetie Pie,

Your mother called me Sunday afternoon to tell me how you are getting on, and she made me very happy when she told me that you had promised to improve in eating. So, I don't want you to be too thin, there's no need to be too stout, but if you want to be just right, there is a way to bring it about!

You eat cereal for breakfast, and maybe even an egg
And when they feed you chicken, you ask for the wing or the leg
You love to eat your Jell-O, pudding is sweet as a dream
And even if it happens once a week, you gobble up all the ice cream!
So next time mommy sees you, I just can hear you say
"I feel and eat much better, in every sort of way"

By the way, I am also glad that you like the new Nancy Drew book. I hope you will like your lessons also, as you always do.

I shall write again soon.

A houseful of love,

Aunt Sadie

November 24
1941

To the Fairest Queen Miss Rhoda Levine,

There comes a soldier to do her bidding
He means business and that's no kidding
He will show her how to fight for all that's true, for all that's right
But not to fight with blow or gun
That's how the greatest battles are won!

Yes ma'am. Some people think that a fight means getting all angry and excited, and yelling very loud. Then maybe some punches are exchanged, or people call each other names that are not very nice. In the end, of course, nobody really wins because there wasn't anything really important to fight about in the first place. But sometimes there is something real to fight for. For example, if somebody is ill, it is very important for him to get well again. If it's a girl, the same thing is true. Of course, she will not yell and scream and get all red in the face because she wants to get well again. Do you know how she will fight for her health? She will eat nicely and sleep well, and make believe that she is a queen, always being a wonderful example to those who may be near her. She will be kind, patient and considerate. She will smile much more often than anyone else and the first thing you know she will be getting better and stronger each day.

Hurrah for the Queen!

Love,

Aunt Sadie

NOVEMBER 25
1941

My dear Honey Child,

> Where does the sunlight come from? From over the hill.
> Where does the sunlight go to? To children who smile,
> and once in a while, rest and lie still.
> Where do the moonbeams come from? From 'way out there.
> Where do the moonbeams go to? To light up the
> way, when done is the day, everywhere
> I love the sun and the moonlight, do you love them too?
> Though I love them well, it's a secret, don't tell!
> Best of all, I love only you!

So my dear Rhoda, how do you like that? Pshaw! I can hear you say that you knew it all the time.

Your mother is coming to see you on Wednesday, and of course I just know you are going to greet her with a great big smile. I wonder if she's going to bring you any more books.

My, my! Isn't it wonderful to have beautiful surprises?

Thousands of hugs and kisses.

Aunt Sadie

November 26
1941

Beautiful Lady,

Your mommy was happy when she phoned today,
what wonderful things I heard her say
She made my head spin, and dance and whirl, for
you've become friends with the next-door girl!
You do well in your lessons of course, that being out of school is not a great loss,
Your cheeks are rosy, and smiley too, now what else could I ask of you.
You are eating much better, 'tis plain to see, for the
doctor says "improvement," quite readily
You're having lots of fun, I should merrily say,
especially getting letters every single day!

So, keep up the good work, and also the looks, live nobly and well as they do in your books, and lady, dear lady, I'm sure you'll soon find you're healthy and strong both in body and mind.

There's a silly poem on the next page. Please turn over. (I mean turn over the page, not you.)

Sprinkles on my charlotte, Sprinkles on my cone
I wonder if they'll ever grow, sprinkles on my phone

So! You want to read all of the Nancy Drew mystery books! Do you expect to be a lady detective when you grow up, I had better watch out or I won't be able to surprise you anymore. You will know everything in advance.

Love and kisses,

Aunt Sadie

November 27
1941

My dear little Sunflower,

How is your smile today? You see I never tire of this question because I know deep down in my heart that the answer is a pleasant one. Do you like the joke books Donald* sent you?

I know a place where the sun is like gold, and the cherry blooms burst with snow,
And down underneath is the loveliest nook, where the four-leaf clovers grow.
One leaf is for hope, and one is for faith, and one is for love, you know,
And G-d put another one in for luck, if you search you will find where they grow.
But you must have hope and you must have faith,
you must love and be kind and so,
If you work, if you wait, you'll find the place, where the four-leaf clovers grow!

Do you remember this song? It isn't new, but I thought it would be fun to think of it once in a while.

Poems and songs as you can see, are welcome gifts for a child like me,
Thankful am I in this land to be, where thoughts may be shared quite merrily
When I grow up, I do declare, there'll be many thoughts that I shall share,
Without any fuss, I'll show my devotion, by sharing
my thoughts with the children here,
And also, those children across the ocean!

So, Rhoda, there's some work for you. Begin to think about having beautiful thoughts to give to others. Perhaps you will become a writer someday. We will think about this some more.

A houseful of love,

Hugs and Kisses

Aunt Sadie

---
* Donald was Rhoda's cousin and Uncle Morris's son.

November 28
1941

To my dear little Birdie,

> I saw pigeons feeding on the steps of a church, always
> contented yet always they search.
> A symbol of peace is the gentle dove, and close to G-d, in His infinite love
> I learned a lesson with any guess, from the silent pigeons upon the steps,
> That I might also continue to seek how to be gentle and patient and meek
> I stood on the sidewalk and watched them all, in their
> pretty feathers against the gray wall,
> And a wonderful flash came out of the blue, that I
> might share these thoughts with you!

So, I did, and this is it, of course.

Now, your mother and your daddy will be up to see you again on Sunday, and you may be sure that they are looking forward to hearing some very good things about you. Please do your best, as I know you always do, so that they may have good things to say about you, to me!

Love,

Hugs oooo and kisses xxxx

Aunt Sadie

November 29
1941

To my dear Polly-Dolly,

> There is a little parrot who stands upon my shelf,
> And all he does the whole day long is chatter to himself.
> One day he seemed so very sad, as he chirped there so alone,
> That I took him from that parking space, and put him near my phone,
> Now he has learned a new trick, it appears he stands and rests,
> But he really listens to the callers, then gossips to my guests.
> Oh, my green feathered gossipy Polly, I don't what to do
> I gladly would like to put you out, but I'm much too fond of you!

Again, I am looking forward to hearing some very good news from your mother, as she and your daddy will be visiting you.

Did you know that after your mother calls me up I feel just like the parrot. I want to spread all the news to everybody that knows you, and even to some of my friends who do not yet know you, but no doubt they will know you some day.

Don't be surprised if you receive some Christmas cards from some people you do not know at all. They will surely be people who know you through me, so you better be good.

Hugs and kisses,

Aunt Sadie

November 30
1941

My dear little Chickie,

Guess what! Your mother called me up today, that means Sunday, you know, and she surely made me happy. Do you know why? She made me happy because she told me that soon she will be bringing you your hat and coat so that you might be put into the sun and get the wonderful fresh air! That's the kind of news I like to hear.

I am going to get you something for Christmas, but I can't tell you what it is because then it won't be a surprise, and I do want to surprise you. All I can say is that it will be very pretty, and it is something to wear. You may not be able to wear it very much right away, but pretty soon after you get it, you know, not too many weeks, and it will be just nice and lovely.

Christmas is coming, you better be wise, and don't try to discover, the little surprise
But if you can guess what the present may be, I
shan't mind at all, if the joke is on me!
It may be blue, it may be rose, a cap for your knee, or a muff for your nose
It may be big, and it may be small, perhaps it won't be anything at all.

But, my dear Rhoda, do not worry about it. I know you won't anyway. Have good thoughts!

Loads of love,

Aunt Sadie

It is December

No, it is not No-vember....

1
1941

My dear little Jou-Jou,

Every month new flowers appear, bringing fresh fragrance and giving us cheer,
But the month with its flowers that I hold most dear,
is the month of December, the last in the year
I love the Poinsettias in yellow and red, the mistletoe bough placed over my head,
The tall Christmas trees, the wreaths and the holly,
December's the time to be good and feel jolly.

Indeed, the wintry air will feel very sweet to you, my dear Rhoda, so if they are ready to let you get the warmth of the sunshine, and the crispy kiss of the autumn-y-wintry breezes during the month of December, that is another thing to enjoy this month.

On my desk is a bottle of ink, I look at the bottle, I sit here and think,
It may seem queer, but it really is true, I think about what I write to you.
And when I feel my thoughts are done, I write them down, yes, one by one,
And strangest of all it takes much less time, to write
you my thoughts in this kind of rhyme.

I love you! Hurrah!

Thousands of kisses,

Aunt Sadie

Here are hugs, ooooooooo

December 2
1941

My dear little Peaches and Cream!

Two dainty flowers in a green vase, each of them has a bright shining face,
Yellow cornflowers each on a stem, do they wonder what I think of them?
I think they are lovely, graceful and fair, I'm thankful
to someone for putting them there,
And if they could speak, I'm sure they would say,
"Dear child, may you have all your wishes today."

And believe me, my dear Rhoda, I would join the cornflowers and wish that you may find all your wishes come true <u>every</u> day. That would be something! But your mother will be seeing you on Wednesday, and no doubt your daddy will too, so that's nice. I'm waiting to hear some more good news about you.

A lady lost her hat, she looked so funny, running
quickly like a bunny, to get back her hat.
But it was pressed flat, it wasn't so funny, it costs lots
of money, now what do you think of that!

Lots of love,

Aunt Sadie

December 3
1941

My dear little Apple-Turnover,

*They dress me up warm in my hat and my coat, and
tuck me in close, for my bed is a boat,
Then they row me out, far, far into the sea, but I like the ocean and sail merrily.
My boat's on a porch (I pretend it's a dock), and
though it's quite still, I pretend it can rock.
Then down comes the sunshine, and kisses my cheek,
I'll be healthy and strong in less than a week!
Now deeply I breathe, for I love the cool air, it makes
me feel happy and snappy and fair.
Then back in my bed I go sailing again, it's time once more for the lessons to begin.
I love my lessons, I love my boat,
But best I love my hat and my coat.*

So, you see, Rhoda, your mother has been giving me some good news again. That is why I felt I <u>must</u> write about your hat and coat, and the new way you are going to use it. It really is a lot of fun if you can make believe your bed is a boat. Robert Louis Stevenson used to do it, so why can't you?

I'll write again soon,

Aunt Sadie

ooooxxxxx

December 4
1941

To my dear little Soldier Girl,

There's very much more in being ill, then merely taking medicine, or maybe a pill,
I mean there is much that one may learn, to help us
be better, when strength shall return.
When everyone's quiet at the end of the day, we learn
what it means to think and to pray,
We learn of the wonderful power of love, of vision,
and faith that mountains may move
And when medicine and pills are done, and we are strong and well,
There's many an interesting story, we may have to tell.
Stories may be written in a book or a letter, but only in life can we live much better.

I am wondering if you understand what I am trying to tell you in this little poem. Shall I explain it to you? It simply means that if you are ill there are many things which you cannot do at that time, but there are many things which can happen in your mind that could not possibly happen while one is not quiet. Such things have to do with the kind of thoughts a person has. Beautiful thoughts make a beautiful character; nobody's character is so beautiful that it cannot become even more perfect.

This has been a grown-up letter, when you grow up, you'll like it better, so
Save it my dear, don't throw it away, and you'll read it again some other day.

Oceans of love,

Aunt Sadie

December 5
1941

To my dear little Sunflower,

> Today it was a muggy day, a fuzzy, wuzzy, puggy day, with fog and mist the whole day long.
> For me it was a jolly day, a happy, flappy holiday, with fun and laughs the whole day long.
> Now do you wonder why 'twas so, because of course I'll let you know,
> Good thoughts, good deeds, have made me sing,
> Now a little bit you know, of what has helped make it so,
> And that is what kind deeds will bring.

It does not depend upon the weather, that we are happy or not. It depends upon our own selves. If we think of beautiful things and how we can make other people happy, we become even happier ourselves. Then it does not matter to us whether the sun is shining or not because we have a lot of sunshine with us.

> Sunflower, sunflower, smile upon me,
> That I may learn also a sunflower to be.

Did you know that Christmas is less than three weeks off? I don't know what to do about you. You don't tell your mother what you would like me to get you, and so how can I know? After all, I don't know what children like, do I? So, don't be surprised if you don't get anything from me, and it won't be my fault either.

Love and kisses, kisses and love,

Aunt Sadie

December 6 1941

My dear little Banana Fritter (yum-yum, you taste good!)

Oh, what are aunties here for, here for, here for?
Oh, what are aunties here for, do tell me Maiden fair!
They're here to tell us stories, stories, stories
They're here to tell us stories, and chase away all care
What stories do they tell you, tell you, tell you
What stories do they tell you, that makes you love them so?
That is very easy, easy, easy
That is very easy, you very soon will know.
Mystery stories, and stories for fun, there are stories with rhythm and rhyme,
Bible stories of battles long won, and stories to fill up our time.
That is why we love our aunties, and there are many reasons more
But I cannot tell you now, dear, for there's someone at the door!

Is it true that the children are allowed to see movies once a week? I think that is very lovely.

Hugs and kisses,

From the story Auntie

December 7, 1941

My dear little Mayflower!

I was so happy all day after seeing you. Believe me, I was very lucky to be allowed to come up. Do you know why I was so joyful? It was because you were so smiley and cheerful, and you continue to have your very sweet disposition. Please keep it up. Also continue to do your best with your lessons. I think your English, your spelling and your handwriting are positively beautiful. If your arithmetic problems are a little more difficult, don't you worry. I am sure that later on Sylvia or I will be able to explain any problem to you, and in the meantime you have a very good teacher anyway. I am so glad you are in the play, too.

Oh yes, there is one more thing I must say to you. I shall remember your promise and my promise about the lipstick. Since you have promised not to use Gloria's lipstick anymore, I shall remember my promise and get one especially for you, as soon as I can.

The idea about keeping the letters in a scrapbook later on is an excellent idea.

Many white arms with hearts of gold, have each
of the daisies which my hands hold,
I put them in my vase so blue, and remember the love which I hold for you!

A trainload of love,

Aunt Sadie

P. S. Soon there will be more Christmas poetry coming from me to you. Wait.

December 8
1941

My dear Tootsie-Wootsie,

Oh, my Christmas shopping, my Christmas shopping, when will it ever get done?
I dream of being all finished, but I have not even begun!
There's a stamp-book for a nephew, a bed-jacket for a certain niece,
The baby wants a rocking horse, her cousin wants Traffic Police.
I think I'll bring them bon-bons, to sprinkle upon the toys,
I'll drop some butterscotch on the drum, to be sure it makes enough noise.
I hope they'll like their presents, I hope you'll like yours too,
But since it's no longer a secret, I'll have to get something more for you!
Oh, my Christmas shopping, my Christmas shopping, when will it ever get done?
I dream of being finished, but I have not even begun!

Yes, my dear Rhoda, now that the surprise is known, I shall have to get you something else in addition to <u>it</u>. Isn't that awful? No? You don't think it is? I can see you laughing. Well, I don't care. I'm going to surprise you anyway.

If you want anything, don't be afraid to ask the nurses for it. The main thing is that you should ask for it in a nice way, and I am sure they will not refuse to let you have it, especially if it is good for you, like a blanket, for instance, when you are cold.

A birdie peeped through my window one morning, and said
"Arise, I'm giving you warning, if you don't make haste you'll be late today,"
Then he flapped his wings and he flew away.

Does the little canary ever talk to you? Tweet-tweet, tweet-tweet?

Love,

Aunt Sadie

P. S. Tomorrow I shall write you about the canary

OOOOOOOOOOXXXXXXXXXXXXX

December 9
1941

My dear little Songbird,

As I promised yesterday, I am going to give you something about the little canary. You are really very lucky to have such a jolly companion. Of course I do not mean to belittle Gloria. She is even more than a jolly companion, I am sure. Wouldn't you like to give the birdie a name? How do you like "Pudgy"?

A canary was swinging close near my bed, "tweet-tweet, twitter-tweet, to-woo."
He hopped around, skipped about over my head,
"tweet-tweet, twitter-tweet, to-woo."
One day I tried to hear what he said, "tweet-tweet, twitter-tweet, to-woo."
From a book in my hand I suddenly read, "sweet-sweet, be my sweet, you-hoo."
And now as he sings when he perks his dear head, I
look at him wisely, from out of my bed,
I remember the day when I leisurely read, and
understood clearly, the words when he said,
"Sweet-sweet, be my sweet, you-hoo."

Here is another one for Pudgy:

Dear canary bird, shut in a cage, you do not fuss, or fume or rage,
You are content to sing all the day, and make lovely music in your own sweet way.
Your feathers are yellow, and bright in the sun, you
never grow tired, you never are done,
But to all who can hear you, to girl or to boy, you bring a wonderful earful of joy.
They take you away when at last it is night,
and you stop your singing, "'cause there is no more light,"
But I know in the morning again you shall start
So, thank you, dear birdie, with all of my heart.

Aunt Sadie

xxxxxxxxxxoooooooooo

December 10
1941

My dear little Apple-Blossom,

What wonderful news from your mother I had today! Do you know how happy you made me? No? Well, it made me very happy to hear that you are doing so nicely and that the good treatment has begun. I am sure you must have been glad to see your grandpa too.

How is the Christmas play getting along[?] By the way, Sunday is Donald's birthday and your mother is getting a card for him which you are going to send the next time she sees you. Isn't that thoughtful of your mother. My goodness, how she must love you! And your daddy, too.

A beautiful picture hangs on my wall, which never has spoken a word at all,
And yet as it stands eternally still, it has a great message for all to fulfill
There is a figure with folded hands, who hears all our problems and understands.
There is a vase in lovely pale gold, where rose-white Magnolias gently unfold.
And off in the distance, all through the day, the
horizon is misty in pink, blue and gray.
What, in its silence, does this picture tell, mysterious
background, yet clear as a bell?
I know what it says, all its days without end, there is
nothing as dear as the heart of a friend.

Love,

Aunt Sadie

December 11
1941

My dear little Lotus Blossom,

> I have a pretty mirror that is round and bright and shiny,
> The only fault that I can find is that the glass is much too tiny,
> And when I look into its face to see how my new hat goes,
> I'm very lucky if I can find the tip of my fat little nose!
> When I am grown up, I declare, though some may think me vain,
> I shall have a looking glass as big as a window pane,
> So that I may view myself complete, even in full-length clothes,
> And scorn the tiny round mirrors that reflect but the tip of my nose!

Do you know what is the most wonderful thing in the world? I was going to give you the answer, but on second thought, why should we not make a game out of it? Let's pretend that it is a riddle. Think about it, guess the answer, if you can, and tomorrow I shall tell you what it is.

Hint: It makes bad people good, sick people well, and it has four letters.

Love,

Aunt Sadie

December 12
1941

My dear little Lovebird,

Are you feeling "fit as a fiddle"? Do you know the answer to that riddle? I am listening, please tell it to me.

Yes, that's it, L-O-V-E.

And that, my dear Snooky, is the Greatest Thing in the World. Don't you think so, too?

> *The wind is whistling through the trees,*
> *as loudly and freely as ever you please,*
> *He is glad of his work as he makes the leaves fall,*
> *and spins them around like I spin my ball.*
> *All through the night I can hear the wind blow,*
> *he's promising me that he'll bring on the snow,*
> *I know that it's fun to ride on my sled,*
> *but at night, when it's cold may I stay a-bed?*

I sent Donald "The Arabian Nights," for his birthday, which is on Sunday. Your mother will bring you a card to send to him, if she doesn't forget. Here's another one about the wind.

> *The frisky wind is biting my toes*
> *He's slapping my cheeks and pinching my nose,*
> *But he tickles my head when he slides through my hair,*
> *I like the sharp wind, and I call him "Fresh Air."*

So, you see, it all depends on how you look at things. Sometimes you don't like something, like the wind, for instance, and at another time you <u>do</u> like the same thing. How do <u>you</u> feel?

I never drank tomato juice and so I couldn't stand it. But now I am so used to this that daily I demand it!

My, oh my, is that so?

Love as ever,

Aunt Sadie

DECEMBER 13
1941

My dear little Buttercup,

Today I had so much fun, I went shopping in the rain. Guess what I went shopping for? Did I get it? Well, I guess I did, and my, oh my, what a pretty one it is!

Pitter-patter the rain came down, as I went rambling all over town,
Christmas is the time for fun, but I am glad that now my shopping's begun.
The rain is splashing on my face, it makes me feel wonderfully clean,
It nurtures the flowers on my Father's place,
What does a rainstorm mean?
It means that calmness, soon will be here,
The fruit and the flowers will grow,
Let us live and laugh without any fear,
G-d cares for us all here below.

Yes, it is certainly good to know that somehow, we always get exactly what we need, although it is sometimes a little hard to understand this.

Love and laughter,

Aunt Sadie

December 14
1941

My dear little Water-Lily,

I spoke to Donald only a little while ago. He told me that he has been enjoying his birthday. He went to the movies, and received books and other presents. He asked for you and so did Gladys. Donald was very happy when I told him you had sent him a birthday card. So, you see, even if you are far away, you can make other people happy.

When your mother spoke to me over the phone Sunday afternoon, she told me you had been in the electric pool last Thursday. I was very glad to hear that you like it. I told you that your bed was a boat! Do you remember? In one of my poems?

> *Two little girls with rosettes in their hair, sit all day with an occupied air,*
> *They read all day, these two little tots, each near a basket of forget-me-nots*
> *With a book on her lap and a smile on her face,*
> *neither one or the other moves an inch from her place.*
> *Although they came together, as twins always do,*
> *They face opposite directions, yet are quite contented too.*
> *Each sister is demure as she simply sits and looks,*
> *For they both are trying very hard to hold up a row of books,*
> *It isn't really difficult to keep on being friends,*
> *If you're only made of porcelain and they use you for bookends.*

This poem is something of a riddle too. Could you guess what I was talking about before I got the very end of it all. Yes, these are bookends on my very own bookcase in my very own room.

Love and kisses,

Aunt Sadie

December 15
1941

To my dear little Bringer-of-good-Tidings,

> This has been a perfect day, for it started in a perfect way
> If I said no more, I'm sure you'd guess what added to my happiness
> What could make me finer, how could I feel better
> Then, by receiving a certain welcome letter?
> So, whenever, you have time and don't know what to do,
> A letter is the very thing to be written up by you!

Yes, indeed I prize the letter which you wrote. "Love" is the answer to the riddle. You guessed it alright.

By the way, Claire* feels fine and is very happy that you remember her. Please give my best greeting to Gloria. As for the lipstick, I am afraid I must ask you once again to be patient. It is not a very good thing to send in the mail because it may get crushed; besides when you do get it, I should like to show you the right way to put it on. In the meantime, I am sure there are more interesting things to think about.

For instance, the writing of poetry. I was very glad to learn that you like my little poems, but I do not understand why you say that you cannot write some too. Have you tried? You know, in the beginning it need not be more than two lines, if you wish. I think if you can write such a lovely letter as you wrote to me, then you can write other things also. To be sure it may take some time, but it is worth it.

Gracious me! I didn't know this was going to be such a long letter. Well, I have an idea about the poetry. When you come home, as you are saving the poems, we will go over them together. You will tell me which ones you like the best. Then I will type them out, and make them into a book. Then I shall ask one of my friends to make pictures for some of the poems,

---

* Claire was a friend of Sadie's.

perhaps for the one about the Canary, and you will help me to get some nice titles. Perhaps then we can go to a publisher and then printed into a real book. Wouldn't that be wonderful? Anyway, think about it.

With beautiful thoughts and love for you,

Aunt Sadie

December 16 1941

My dear little Early-Bird,

I have a little friend, and he has a happy face,
And oh, he goes so very fast though he stands in one place,
But when he has to stay at home and hasn't much to do,
He hardly moves his hands around, and dear, he looks so blue!
I feel so awfully sorry when Mr. Clock goes slow,
His arms I know are heavy but around they must go,
Yes there's a way I can help to keep him right in step,
It's by keeping busy all the while and being full of pep.
Tick-tock, Mr. Clock, your troubles now are done,
I shall think of many ways to keep you on the run.

This poem, I'm afraid, is not so very good, but I shall work it some more, and perhaps re-write it. There is really very much that may be said about a clock.

I have keys to my cellar, I have keys to my door,
But if I had the cookie jar key, I wouldn't ask for more.

Another poem:

Sweet little angel forever you kneel, do you know the things I feel?
Do you know my thoughts are true, as you pray for me and I think of you?
Thank you, sweet angel, you're a good omen,
You have brought me joy since that evening when
My dear friend Irene, through loving and living,
Bequeathed you to me on the Day of Thanksgiving.

P. S. This poem is true. My friend Irene gave me a little angel statue on Thanksgiving Day.

Love,

Aunt Sadie

December 17
1941

To my dear little Wide-eyed Maid,

Your mother called me today (Wednesday), and again she told me very encouraging news about you. The doctors and the nurses like you very much. They think you are very cooperative and that you have a very joyful spirit. That is how I should like you to be always. Yesterday I did not like one of the poems at all, so I decided to try again, on the same subject, and here it is:

I have a little friend who has a jolly face,
And when he's feeling very good, he runs at a lively pace;
But when he's feeling grumpy, and hasn't much to do,
He moves as slow as molasses, and his face gets long and blue
When he's very busy, he swigs his arms around,
And if you listen very hard, you can hear his rickety sound;
But when he is neglected, his hands grow heavy till,
He gets all exhausted, and then he stands still.
Sometimes in the morning, before the birdies sing,
My friend decides with himself that he had better ring,
Then he begins a tantrum, and I get quite a shock,
To find I've been alarmed again by my dear friend Mr. Clock!

When you have time, and feel like it, perhaps you can think up some good titles for some of the poems I am sending you. By the way, I forgot to tell you that when the book of poems will be published, I shall write in the beginning of it, something like this: "Dedicated affectionately to my Dear Niece Rhoda."

Love,

Aunt Sadie

December 18
1941

My dear little Christmas Carol,

Of course, you must be thinking very much about Christmas by this time, and all about Santa Claus. Oh, yes, my dear little Christmas Wishy, how is the play getting on.

> *Yellow snapdragons, and roses red,*
> *While Christmas carols ran through my head*
> *Mountain pink and a low cloud of fern*
> *Made an unusual picture which oft shall return*
> *I know that often, in days to come*
> *I shall have need to remember some of the music I heard tonight*
> *"Victory music, and "Holy Night," then I shall be glad that I can review*
> *The lovely evening, by sharing with you!*

If you have not yet received a letter or a card from Claire, I want to tell you that you may possibly receive something in the mail. Claire was very happy that you thought of her.

Keep on being cheerful, as I keep on loving you.

Aunt Sadie

ooooooooo

xxxxxxxxx

December 19
1941

My dear little bundle of Christmas Cheer,

This evening I looked out the window of my office because I heard a strange sound and what do you suppose I saw?

> I saw a tall Christmas tree planted in the sunken garden
> and on its branches, huge balloons in red and white
> Swayed gently in the breezes of the evening casting on the icy ground a sacred light
> A choir of men and women, gathered in pavilion sang
> Christmas carols, hymns of long ago
> And they looked like a host of G-d sent angels, as on
> their upturned faces, softly fell the snow
> Thankfully my heart rejoiced within me as I
> thoughtfully looked down upon the scene
> Knowing well that fortune smiles upon us bringing
> many blessings, inner joys serene
> Then let us banish any care or sorrow that may hover over heart or mind
> Let us bring to one another Christmas spirit, for by
> bringing joy, our happiness we find

So, what do you think? After hearing the men and women singing these pretty songs I went home, and spent time in my chorus too. We are having a Christmas party for my friends at the hotel, and I, together with a few others are in the chorus. Tonight, we had a rehearsal. We will have another rehearsal on Monday. Wednesday night we are having the party. We sing "Silent Night," "Jingle Bells," "Old King Cole," and other songs. Someday you and I shall sing them together.

Love,

Aunt Sadie

December 21
1941

My dear little Amazon,

What is this wonderful news I am hearing about you? Your mother tells me you are moving your legs in a new way as never before! Keep it up!! That is wonderful!!

I am anxious to see the new rooms also. That means you and I shall both be very patient, and soon we shall see the new home. Imagine, now you shall probably have your radio in your very own room. And isn't it also very wonderful to know that after you have been home for a while, you may go away with your mother and Larry again to the country? I shall come up to visit you for a weekend or so.

I suppose you are all prepared for your Christmas play. Your mother is <u>very</u> glad of the opportunity to be able to see you an extra time, of course. I was busy shopping on Saturday, and br-r-r-r, was it cold! Today is so cold, too. By the way, Claire told me today (Sunday), that she sent a card. I think that is a very fine thought, she is very busy, and it is kind of her to think of you. You will probably receive the card on Monday, if you have not yet received it.

Who is knocking at my door?
Who is blowing misty breath upon my window pane?
He has knocked here once before
He has blown, been gone, and come again.
I know him, you know him, we all love him, too
He was with us, and then got lost,
he plays with me, he plays with you,
He laughs when we call him Jack Frost

Jack Frost can't come through my door,
Nor through my window pane,
I play with him only on the street
And there we shall play again.

Love,

Aunt Sadie

December 22
1941

To the dearest little Actress in the world,

I just know you are going to do well in the play because I remember hearing about how successful you were in the "Dearest Maiden," or was it the "Snow Maiden." Your mother is going to call me up afterwards and tell me all about it. So, Good Luck!

> A Christmas tree, a tall evergreen, the prettiest one I ever have seen,
> Dressed up from top to toe, rooted in a bank of snow,
> Is standing in my room.
> There are hundreds of lights in red, blue and pink,
> that smile at me, and then they wink,
> For deep down in the bank of snow, the lights and I, very well know
> What's standing in my room.
> There are presents, yes, many gifts, hidden in the make-believe snow drifts,
> There are toys for the children and me, as anyone at all can see,
> Hiding in my room.
> So, while the tinsel is crinkling, and the star atop is twinkling,
> The Christmas bell is softly tinkling, melodies of joy;
> To all of us sweet Christmas joy
> Is hiding in my room.

So, I do hope you will find a great deal of Christmas joy, and lots of reason to be merry. Be sure to keep smiling on Christmas Day, just as you do every day. Make all your little neighbors happy, mostly by being really joyful yourself deep inside. This kind of joy does not mean that we must make a lot of noise. Oh, no, but we spread warmth and love and sunshine, <u>silently</u>.

So much love,

Aunt Sadie

December 23
1941

To my dear little Star Actress,

Mother called me and told me how very much she enjoyed seeing you do the play so well. Also, the nurse who gives you your exercises thinks your improvement is just wonderful! Keep it up.

>It's fun to be in a Christmas play,
>And help to chase people's troubles away;
>But even in real life, all through the year,
>I can bring laughter, good-will, and good cheer.

Love,

Aunt Sadie

CHRISTMAS EVE 24
1941

My dear little Lambkins,

Tonight, we had our Christmas party. I wore my evening gown, and I was in a chorus together with some of my friends. It was really very nice. We sang "Silent Night," "Jingle Bells," "Old King Cole," and also Brahms' "Lullaby," and "Come All Ye Faithful." The room was beautifully decorated with pines and pine cones, and of course, there was the Christmas tree.

Did I tell you that I received a letter from Donald?

Tomorrow, (I mean on Friday) I may visit Sylvia, Alvin and Gorgie.**

Love,

Aunt Sadie

---

* Rhoda's cousins and Uncle Harry's children. "Gorgie" is Loretta.

Christmas Day
25
1941

My dear little Plum Pudding,

>Hodge-podge-smudge-nudge, see-saw-say
>My table's in a jumble this merry Christmas Day,
>All the goodies, toys and gifts my friends have given me,
>I placed upon my table when I took them off the tree!

Another Poem:

>Forest pine needles crisscrossed on the wall,
>Bend in simplicity to scent and grace the hall
>Crunchy brown pine cones scattered here and there
>Add a festive, joyous spirit to the crisp December air.
>Oh, pine needles, pine cones, please whisper to me
>Why these songs and dances around the Christmas tree?
>Pine tree, you are old and wise, while I am but a child,
>None but I shall hear the story as your tone is soft and mild.
>The pine tree told the story that is old and yet ever new,
>I listened very carefully, and so I wiser grew,
>Then I kissed the pine tree's branches, lo its fragrance clung to me,
>And next morning I awakened with a new love for the tree.

Another Poem:

>Two tall candles burning bright,
>Illuminated the table where I ate tonight
>While a bunch of narcissus, gold, white and true
>Made me think for a long while, of you!

With love,

Aunt Sadie

December 26
1941

My dear little Ducky-Wucky,

I have so much to tell you tonight! Where shall I begin? I have just come back from visiting Alvin, Sylvia, and the baby. She is very sweet and clever. They all asked about you, and send you their very best love.

Alvin and Sylvia want me to tell you that they think about you often. They also want to write to you, but they do not know what to write about. Aunt Jean and Uncle Harry send the best of their love. You will be able to see them all fairly soon.

I bought Alvin a new top, and two little books for Gorgie, and some candy for Sylvia.

How has the mail been coming on these days? One day I could not get stamps, and although I had the letters written I could not send them to you. Then, of course, as you know, the Christmas mail is always very heavy.

By the way, I shall be visiting your mother and Larry on Saturday. Then, Saturday night, I shall write and tell you all about the new rooms. I shall describe it all to you. Won't that be nice?

<u>*The Mailman*</u>

Every day the mailman rings,
With a great leather pack, slung over his back
Welcome messages he brings
Every day I sit and wait
With a song and a smile, I hope all the while,
He will not today be late
Rain or shine he never fails,
With hellos for us all, the big and the small

Bringing love thoughts in the mails
Oh, how thankful I must be
In my own silent way, that also I may
Serve through waiting patiently.

Another Poem:

My friend goes scribble-dee-dee
And soon there is a letter for me,
I go doodle-dee-doo,
And here is a letter for you!

I shall write again tomorrow.

Love and kisses,

Aunt Sadie

December 27
1941

My dear little Tulip,

> Gracious me!
> You might want to see, what I have seen today.
> The rooms so new, with quite a view, that stretches far away.
> There are arches and nooks, and shelves for your books,
> Of closets I think there are five, there are knick-knacks and bric-bracs,
> And tucked away towel racks, sunny windows to help us to thrive
> Another new treat, is a five cornered street,
> Which is easily seen from a well-arranged seat, that shall help the hours to fly
> It is all up to date, in a first-class state,
> So, it's very worthwhile to joyfully wait, even as had to do I!

Yes, my darling. When I came to the new rooms today, mother had left me a note. She was out with Larry shopping. So, I stood downstairs and waited. The neighborhood is very nice, and this house is the nicest one on the five (or six) corners. It is called "King Oakes." Isn't that odd?

There is some shrubbery in the front of the house and a small courtyard. There is a large warm lobby, with pictures painted on the walls, and a rug on the floor. You go up on the elevator and then turn right. It is on the third floor. You come in to a large foyer which has two arches. The foyer has wall paper of a gay garden pattern. It is excellent to play in. It is also good to play in the spacious living room which is painted a pale blue. This room has the good rug on the floor, and there are large built in book shelves. All windows have venetian blinds. The kitchen is tiny, but everything fits in perfectly. It is painted white, and your daddy has bought the most adorable curtain rods, and flowered curtains are hanging at the window. The bathroom has a built-in clothes hamper, and a clothes dryer. It is between your room and your mother's. Your room is sunny and larger than the last room you had. Your mother's room is very large, and there is the window at which you can sit and see the busy street, and wave to me when I come.

I told you all this to make you happy, and because I know you will continue to be cheerful and patient for a while longer until you are ready to come home.

Love,

Aunt Sadie

[Author's note: I am amazed at how well my great-aunt described this home, which was actually an apartment. It is the apartment where I visited my grandparents until they passed away. Reading this brings back so many happy memories, and she describes it exactly how I remember it. My cousins and I would sit at that window in my grandmother's room and watch that busy street, listening to the sirens of passing police cars. We loved to count how many convertible cars would come rambling by. We played in that lobby, which was huge, and that outdoor courtyard. It was a wonderful time.]

December 28
1941

My dear little Butter-nose,

Larry plays the fiddle, Alvin plays the drum,
Gorgie marches 'round the room, while I look on and hum
First, they play at soldiers, then sailors out to sea,
But I don't care at what they play, as long as they play with me.

Mother called me up today, and told me what a bunch of presents you received. She and your daddy had their hands full carrying the things home. You certainly are a popular young lady. I should like to be home with you when you open all these gifts again.

Mommy also told me about your improvement, and of course I am very, very happy. However, now is the time when you have to be very careful. It is wonderful that you are able to turn over on your tummy, or to sit up by leaning on your elbow, but, I hope your mother explained to you that it's much, much better, and in fact, it is very important that you should wait just a little longer until the doctor and nurses gives you permission to do so.

As I know you love me, I know also that you will happily practice patience still a little longer. Soon, very soon, you will be allowed.

I can wait a little longer, till I have become much stronger,
Rejoicingly I wait and smile, for soon, I know, I'll walk a mile.
Not only outer strength I'm winning, now also my character is beginning
To be molded, firmer, true, and of life I get a broader view.
Who can guess that a little child, meek as I, humble and mild,
Have learned so much that adults don't dream,
And so, I am happier than it may seem.

oooooo

xxxxxxx

Aunt Sadie

January 1
1942

My dear young Lady,

Happy New Year to you!
I feel like a very bad girl because I skipped writing to you for two days. However, I have been thinking about you constantly, and I heard from your mother again. I shall have to make this a long letter to take the place of two letters, you know.

Well, I certainly was very glad to hear that Miss Baum thinks you will be allowed to sit up soon. We shouldn't worry if she doesn't say exactly when! As long as we know it is on the way. Believe me, that is wonderful.

So! Your mother is going to make you good things to eat when you come home! Guess what I am going to do. I shall make chocolate ice cream under your very own nose! Maybe you won't like that! Oh, you will? Then you shall have to help me. I mean you shall have to help me eat it.

Out in the city's busiest street,
From a crack in the sidewalk close to my feet,
Pushing its way where the milling crowds pass,
My wandering eye 'spied a lone blade of grass.
From the side of the curbstone, bravely it grew,
Always in danger though scarcely in view;
I had to speed by, 'twas the noon hour of day,
But I knew in my heart what that lone blade might say.
"Be not easily dismayed, never, never be afraid.
Is your foundation firmly laid? Have your plans in Heaven been made?
Then go ahead, and smile, never fear the maddened crowd,
Raving, waving, long and loud, have you faith in all you do?
Even though known to a few? Then go ahead and smile"
Then in the midday shining sun,
I thought of the Almighty, wonderful one,
Whose hand makes miracles come to pass,
Even when touching a lone blade of grass.

I am going to get you a beautiful, beautiful surprise for your room, which I have been promising you for a long time, yet never carried out. Well, this time it is going to happen. Can you guess?

Last night we had our New Year's Party, which I wrote you about the other day. Unexpected we had a very darling little girl dance for us. Her name is Patricia, and she is about six years old, the niece of one of my friends. She has short blond curls and twinkling blue eyes. Some of the girls dressed her up in a sweet little costume and put a shining red hat on her head with 1942 written on it. We also had a short play called, "Poor Old Jim," which was very funny, especially in one part where the lady made a mistake and said "My poor old Phil," instead of saying "My poor old Jim."

With twinkling toes,
As sweet as a rose,
While Patricia dances,
The Old Year goes out!
The musician strums,
The singer hums,
While Patricia dances,
The New year comes in!

And so, with my very best wishes for your speedy and complete return to health, I love you more than ever.

Aunt Sadie

January 2
1942

My dear little Honeykins,

How is your smile today?

How is your smile when you get surprises? I am planning to find out, by preparing some surprises for you. Now that's all I'm telling!

> *I looked out of my window eight stories high*
> *And, there painted against a colorless sky,*
> *Alone, trembling, aloof, in the garden of a neighboring roof,*
> *A leafless tree struggled for hours, and won,*
> *For then the wind, but not the tree, was done.*
> *Though bereft of adornment, though poor or alone,*
> *There is no need our fate to bemoan;*
> *Courage, humbleness, joy, makes of obstacles a toy;*
> *Real victories are determined by far,*
> *By not how we look, but how we are!*

So, how are you? Of, course I know that you are looking very good too, which makes it all the better. I know because you looked very pretty and sweet the last time, I saw you, and also your mother has been telling me. Do you have ribbons for your hair? Love from Uncle Harry.

Love,

Aunt Sadie

January 3, 1942

My dear little Spongecake,

I can hardly wait to show you the surprise, but I must be careful not to tell you about it. Sh-sh! Mums the word. Did you know that Sylvia's birthday is on Thursday, January 15th? Please be sure to send her a card.

> *The sun sinks behind the river at night,*
> *And we welcome the brilliant electric light,*
> *But he beams by day, I do declare,*
> *To see that he is used everywhere.*

I like this one better:

> *We welcome the brilliant electric light*
> *When the sun drops into the river at night,*
> *But he beams all day,*
> *I do declare to find he is king of Everywhere.*

Did I tell you what I did on New Year's Day? I typed up all the poems I have written to you, which I have saved. Do you know that there are forty-five of them, plus a few which you have? There are more to come, of course, and better ones, too!

Greatest Love,

Estelle

January 4
1942

My dear little Friend,

Does this seem like a very plain name to call you? But, believe me, it is not really simple to be a friend, so it has a very special meaning to me.

First of all, I want to tell you how much I enjoyed visiting you today. I think you are showing great improvement, by what you can do and from what you told us. But if you really want to be my friend, which is more than merely being my niece, you will have to prove it, and so I am going to ask you to do something for me which I know is hard to do, but if you want to be my friend, you will do it.

All day I have been thinking about what you said concerning your food, and so on. Well, now, I do not expect that you should eat anything which tastes absolutely horrid, but I do insist that you should be <u>very</u> nice about it. If any nurse says, "I want you to eat this or that," you must remember that she is being unselfish. She will not get fat from what you eat. But if you eat nicely, you will get strong. But you may say "the food doesn't taste good." As I said before I do not expect you to eat badly cooked food. But could you not say as sweetly as possible, <u>no matter to whom</u> I am sorry Miss ___, I am not used to eating oatmeal (or soup or whatever it is), which is prepared this way.

You see dear, there is a proverb which says, "A soft answer turneth away wrath." Now, I know this is true because I have often practiced it and I want you to practice it also. Perhaps you would not want to do it for yourself, but would it not be easier if you do it while you think of me? I am sure that for my sake, and for my love you can do it.

Remember, the nurses are very busy, and you must cooperate with each one as much as possible, no matter what the other children may do. I am sending you a .03 cent stamp for you to use, whenever you wish. Poems tomorrow!

Love,

Aunt Sadie

January 6
1942

My dear little Egg Sandwich,

Gracious me! What will I be calling you next? I came across something in a book I was reading, and it made me think about what we spoke about on Sunday. I copied it out of the book to give to you. I thought you might like to read these sentences. It has to do with praying and I thought what your mother said was very good, to do as your heart tells you.

Now here is what I copied: "Prayer is only another name for good, clean, direct thinking. When you pray, think well what you are saying and make your thoughts into things that are solid. In that manner, your prayer will have strength and that strength shall become part of you, mind, body and spirit."

Isn't that beautiful? Do you understand it? It means that prayer is not merely a jumble of words, but it is rather the thoughts of kindness that we have in our hearts. For example, you might pray to become strong soon which means you will think about becoming strong and all well, so that you can make many more persons happy by your unselfish deeds. Meanwhile remember that every kind thought you have can bring you more strength, so even if somebody is not very wonderful, it is still more worthwhile to be polite, and <u>very</u>, <u>very</u> cheerful.

I know! It's all my fault!! I should write more funny ones!!! Let me see, now.

My friend who lived in Decatur
Had cheeks as red as a termater
Three times a day, she ate vegetables, yea,
Until she turned into a pertater.

But the one who lived in Crete
Thrived only on bread and cooked meat,
He grew very fat, no wonder in that,
While his face became red as a beet!

Oh, well, Lots of Love from Uncle Morris and Uncle Harry too

Aunt Sadie

January 6
1942*

My dear little Singing-Bird,

<u>The Window Cleaner</u>

The man was simple and humble in mien,
His duty was lowly—my windows to clean,
It was the mid-winter, we shivered from cold,
He threw up the sash, and was firm in his hold
As he washed and wiped all the dirt away,
Light-hearted as a mid-summer's day
He stood on the ledge with a belt 'round his waist,
Then back into the room he came with great haste,
'Twas not fear of the cold that made him move fast,
But the many windows he cleans as a part of his task.
I never had noticed the man before,
But he made me think now, as he closed the door.
How often a friend, by sheer circumstance
Clears the eyes of our soul by a word or a glance,
Then with horizon fresh to our view,
We see old things in a light that is new.

I saw Claire tonight and gave her your thanks. She was very happy and may write to you again.

Today was very cold, br-r-r. You must be glad to be indoors, or do they let you go out on the porch[?] If they do, please be sure to keep your ears and your chest covered, you darling little monkey.

Love,

Aunt Sadie

VICTORY

xxxxxxxxx

---

* There are two letters in the collection dated January 6.

January 7
1942

My dear little Chickadee,

Mother called me up today and I heard some very good news about you again. I am <u>so</u> happy to hear that you are getting along better with—you know who. That certainly is fine. Your mother also told me that you sent her a beautiful letter. Then when I called Uncle Harry, he told me about the very lovely letter you had written to Sylvia. She is going to save it and has already answered you I believe.

Do you know why you are writing such nice letters? Well, it is because you pay attention to your schoolwork and do your lessons. If you will continue, as I know you will of course, I am sure you will write more and more beautifully, because what you write will be enriched by the things you learn in History, in Geography and even in Arithmetic. So, keep up the good work.

By the way, your mother also told me that they have put something on to keep your legs down. Did you know that this is a sign of improvement, and has been made possible only because you cooperate so willingly. Your legs are becoming stronger, so of course, you are moving them around. But they do not want any strain upon the tender muscles whatsoever, so they are using this way to help you keep your tootsie-wootsie still. Good luck to you.

How is Gloria? Give her my best greetings. Did you lend her the book which Sylvia sent you?

Chips and stamps and rubber bands, find their way into my hands,
Unanswered letters, un-finished mail,
May be cause for complaint or a sad, sorry tale.
But excuses have no uses where work is concerned,
Work has to be done; so, I have learned

> *To put rubber bands, clips and such things in their place*
> *And attend to my mail with good cheer and good grace.*
> *So, when at last my desk is clear,*
> *I feel at peace, nor my conscience I fear*

I love you more and more every day, for you are my little scheppseli. (Do you know what that is? No? Then ask your mother. Well, maybe I'll tell you tomorrow!)

Good night,

HURRAY

Aunt Sadie

January 8
1942

Dear little Lambkins,

Yes-m, that's what it means when I call you "my scheppseli." It means my little lamb. I do hope you will forgive me. I did not mail your yesterday's letter until tonight because I didn't have a stamp, but this time I bought two stamps, and this letter will go out tonight without fail.

> *What makes Jack Frost so angry? What makes the cold so blue?*
> *Why does the North wind blow so hard, that the sun can scarcely shine through?*
> *Where have the songbirds hidden, where did they fly away?*
> *Why do the tulips sleep so fast, in the midst of a winter's day?*
> *Hush, hush, Proserpine is sleeping, she sleeps six months in the year*
> *The birds and the flowers who love her, wake only when she is near*
> *Jack Frost may freeze the water, the North wind may constantly blow*
> *But the wee ones are waiting for springtime, when Proserpine helps them grow*

Darling, do you know the story about Ceres and her daughter Proserpine and Demeter? If you know the story, then you will understand the poem I have written. If you do not know the story, please let me know and I shall tell it to you, or write it to you, or get you a book which has it in it.

I love you more and more. Can you tell me why?

COURAGE

Aunt Sadie

January 9
1942

My dear little Daffy-down-dillie,

> *I saw golden Daffodils, and a bird on the wing,*
> *Children of G-d, all heralds of spring.*
> *I saw a bunch of Daffodils on somebody's table,*
> *I would like to spread them far and wide, if only I were able.*
> *I can make the days go by and speed along the hours,*
> *By singing while the birdies fly and talking to the flowers.*
> *I love the yellow Daffodil, the Tulip and the Rose,*
> *The Iris and the Violet, and every flower that grows.*

Isn't it wonderful, my darling? The flower shops are beginning to show more and more spring flowers, and I have such a longing to write about the flowers to you. It is really a little early for spring flowers but I did see Daffodils already. By the way, did you know I am saving the most adorable book for you? It is not a new book, but it is a very delightful one. It contains stories about flowers, in which the flowers are personified. That means that they think and talk and so on. These are stories which I think you would rather have me read to you, and so I am saving the book for some of my future visits to you at home.

Now why do I love you more and more each day?

Aunt Sadie

PATIENCE

January 11
1942

My sweet little Patootie,

What I heard about you today! They took your beautiful anklets off so now you are foot-free again. Well, well, that means it gets better and better. Did you know that Sylvia may come up to see you on Wednesday? That is a nice birthday present, for her to see you, I'm sure. It is very good of her to come up, so be as sweet as you really are and as I know you always are. Next week you may have other visitors. Did your mother tell you? I don't know who it may be, if at all.

My rocking chair is bright, bright red, it stands very close to my little white bed,
I rock to myself—I move to and fro, and soon to slumberland I go.
Mother sings a lullaby tune, daddy will come from his office soon,
I fell fast asleep, and down droops my head, daddy
comes home and puts me in bed.
Quick as a wink, the morning is here, daddy says "you are my sunshine dear,"
He dashes away be it raining and fair, and I am alone with my red rocking chair.

I love you more and more,

Aunt Sadie

LOVE

January 12
1942

My dear little Honeysuckle,

You certainly know how to make a surprise. And what a lovely surprise your letter was! I certainly am glad to hear that you are improving in your exercises, and are making progress in your schoolwork. Do you also have promotions? That would be very fine; but if not, it doesn't really matter. It was very thoughtful of your mother to do something special for your teacher. That blot doesn't look very special does it?* Keep on being friends with Mrs. Torrents, and I'm sure you will not regret it.

Claire is very happy whenever you remember her. Thank you. The other girls send you their best regards also. By this, I mean not only the girls I live with, but also a few girls in my office who know about you. So, you see, you are a very popular young lady. You will have to be very good to deserve having so many people think about you.

> *Picture books are calling, games and chalk and clay,*
> *I can keep on stalling, until the end of the day.*
> *There are unanswered letters lying on my shelf,*
> *Oh, I can build castles, and find many things with which to amuse myself.*
> *But I know it would be wiser, if I should begin at once*
> *To attend to all my lessons, lest I become a dunce!*

Of course, that doesn't mean you, because I know you attend to your lessons. Why do I love you more and more?

CHEERFULNESS

Love,

Aunt Sadie

---

* This is a reference to an accidental inkblot on the word "special."

January 13
1942

My dear little Knicker-Knacker,

The trolley cars are cling-clanging down the street,
I keep time by ding-dangling both my feet,
The autos and the buses are honk-honking their alarms,
I refuse to be outdone so chonk-chonk, go both my arms.
They're busy doing many things out in the street below,
But I am learning many things that no one else can know.
Their time is always taken up with running, shouting, seeing
Yes, I am very satisfied, and very busy being.
The stars peep into my window by night,
When the kindly watchers turn out the light,
I take a wish upon a star,
To learn where the most precious jewels are.
The friendly stars, they whisper to me,
Of beautiful gems and rare treasury,
They guide me till dawn, and when they grow dim,
I've learned that the jewels are hidden within.

Do you understand that last poem? It means that the most precious things are those which are found within yourself. That does not mean somebody's heart or stomach, although these organs are also within one's body. It means those things within such as kindness, gratefulness, love and so on. I think you understand what I mean. I hope Sylvia will visit you on Wednesday, as I mentioned in one of the last letters. Feel good, keep smiling, and you will surely keep on improving.

Why do I love you more and more each day?

EFFORT (Effort means that you are trying, which is very important)

Good bye for tonight,

Love,

Aunt Sadie

January 14
1942

To my dear little Pumpkin,

Some people pay attention, some people pay your fare,
Some people pay you compliments, in essence truly rare.
Others may pay homage, respects perhaps they pay,
But what I treasure most of all, is the visit you paid today.

Now wouldn't that be something cute to write to Sylvia? Yes, I know she visited you with your mother on Wednesday. Afterwards she called me up, I mean she spoke to me when your mother called me up and my, oh my, she was so happy about you. She thinks you are wonderful because you are so cheerful. I wonder if she knows the secret why you look good and are cheerful. Do you know the secret? It is because you are always having <u>good</u>, <u>kind</u> thoughts of others. Keep it up.

Why do I love you more and more?

KINDNESS

Aunt Sadie

January 15
1942

To my dear little Tootsie Roll,

> Once upon a time I couldn't tell time,
> But now I can keep time, and beat time,
> And borrow time, and have a good time,
> I use it lest, I abuse it, I make time, I take time,
> And in the meantime, with the word "time,"
> I manage to write rhyme
> Is this the wrong time, the right time, a long time, or the night time?
> In time, without time, to stop, it's about time!

And so, I mean to tell you that I had a very fine time today (Thursday). Friday is my birthday, and the girls in my office made me a surprise luncheon, which they did on Thursday instead of Friday, in order to surprise me. There were about twelve of us and we enjoyed it all. Of course, we couldn't do much more than eat, because our lunch hour is too short so we didn't <u>have enough time!</u> See?

Honeybunch, I love you more and more each day, why?

COURAGE

Aunt Sadie

January 16
1942

My dear little Tiddle-Dee-Winks,

I am so happy today because it is my birthday. A few girls in my office took me to lunch today, can you imagine both yesterday and today they treated me to a celebration.

I received two corsages, one in the morning, in red roses and white sweet peas, the other corsage which I received at night was all in pink sweet peas, tied with a pink bow. The girl who helps me in my office (her name is Mollie), surprised me with a beautiful bouquet of red roses and at night, at home, they made another little party for me, and in the center of the table there were twelve pink carnations and fern, of course. Now they stand upon my dresser, and they are looking straight at me while I am writing this letter. I received a singing birthday greeting over the telephone from someone I know, who is not in New York, and a number of birthday cards. Last but not least, when I came home from my office, I found the lovely telegram from you and your family. I am enclosing it because I want you to see how nice it is, so that you can imagine how happy I feel, and what a wonderful birthday celebration I am really having.

Pink carnations in a wide-mouthed jar
How can you know how pretty they are?
Smooth, silky pon-pons, though you look frail,
Yet you are known to be hardy and hale.
You stand straight before me, your faces alight,
For you are the last thoughts I shall have tonight,
You come to me in your innocent way,
Adding beauty and joy to my happy birthday.
I gaze at you, gaze at you and try hard to think,

Why I love you so, dressed all in pink
Then all of a sudden, I do declare
It's because of my friends who put you there!

Why do I love you more and more each day?

THOUGHTFULNESS

Aunt Sadie

January 18
1942

My dear little Honey-Bell,

What do you suppose! After I mailed you the last letter containing the carnation, I suddenly remembered that I had forgotten to put in the telegram. However, as it was too late to do anything about it, I decided to send it to you with the next mail, and here it is. Mother called me up today and told me that you are continuing to improve. Was I happy? You can imagine. But of course, don't strain yourself darling, in your great desire to do more.

> Over the hill the chimney smokes black,
> And my eye follows the wreath 'till it disappears
> And mingles with the froth clouds above,
> Then to the puffing chimney I turn back
> What are our dreams but a whiff of smoke
> That disappear in the purified realm of reality,
> And unless we make our dreams, visions with clarity,
> We may find ourselves dashed against walls,
> And our castles broke

Why do I love you more and more?

PURITY

Aunt Sadie

January 19, 1942

My dear little Buzz-Buzz,

> I sail my boat to many lands, my anchor I cast on foreign strands,
> Though wondrous strange the sites I see, yet, the children, I find, are just like me.
> They like to play at make-believe, to dance, to sew and even weave,
> The girls like dolls and cookery, they play "school," and "house," too just like me.
> I wish I could take grown ups by the hand, and lead them through my alien land,
> And show them that other folks where ever they be, live, work and play just like me.
> For if they went on such a tour, they'd learn very much, I'm perfectly sure,
> To help them lie in harmony, with all their neighbors just like me.

Why do I love you so dearly?

HARMONY

Aunt Sadie

January 20
1942

To my dear little Scribe,

Thank you, thank you, thank you, for your very lovely and most welcome letter. How happy it made me you will have to imagine! I also enjoyed your birthday wish to me, and the sweet compliments about the poems.

Guess what! I showed yesterday's poem to May, who is a leader of one of the younger children's groups. It was the poem about traveling to many lands. Well, she liked it so much that she wants to use if for the groups, since they are having an international program. Also, don't forget, I am counting upon you to help me get titles for all of these poems later on. Of course, I mean if you would want to do it together with me. Let me know some time.

Fluffs of cloud in rosy hue,
Change size and shape as they float o'er the hill,
But I prance and dance upon their backs,
And travel to faraway lands,
While I look through my window, and in truth,
I confess I am lying quite still.

Love,

Aunt Sadie

January 21
1942

My dear little Daisy,

From gold-hearted daisies,
In a field of green,
I weave a magic crown
For a loving queen

And this reminds me of a conversation which we once had a long time ago about what it means to have the manners of a queen always. Do you remember? Do you live up to your promise to always remember to act like a queen? That means to be noble and have a kind word, and a kind thought for <u>all those whom you meet</u>, even if they themselves seem to be not so wonderful.

Your mother called me today, and I am so glad to learn that Miss Baum is now making you improve even more, by treating your back. That is very good because, no doubt, you will soon be sitting up.

I sat by the river, and over the way,
Clear in the morn of a mid-winter's day
I saw a city before me arise,
With arms outstretched toward the limitless skies.
The people all hungered o'er the valley and hill,
For the bread of life, which I might fulfill
But the sun flecked floes in the river lay,
Barring my passage over the way,
Deep in my heart I knew it was willed
That my message to them should soon be fulfilled,
Now time is precious, nor may there be less
For I hasten to build my bridges across.

Why do I love you more and more, my little Cherub?

NOBILITY

Aunt Sadie

January 22
1942

My dear little Anemone,

> Let us be friends with the sun and the light,
> And receive what they generously give;
> Thus, we shall taste of the deepest delight
> And learn what it means completely to live.
> These are my brothers, the sun, light and air
> They deserve our cooperation, let us become fully aware
> Of their strengthening power and inspiration.

Another poem:

> I love the smell of the salt sea air,
> For when I sniff it, ho-de-ho,
> I think of the places where the big boats go.
> I think of the sailor who hasn't a care,
> Of the wharves and the docks and the many 'hings
> That a good ship sailing the sea-foam brings
> It's loads of fun to float everywhere,
> And the charm of the sea might lure me away,
> But they love me at home, so I can't stow away.

Why do I love you more and more each day?

HONESTY

Love,

Aunt Sadie

January 25
1942

Dearest Darling,

(Am I spoiling you by calling you so many different pet names?)

Please do forgive me for not writing for a day or two, but I have had an extremely busy weekend. Perhaps I shall tell you about it when I see you. I shall certainly do my very best to see you as soon as I possibly can. Meanwhile, do your very best to get better, and better every day. You know that this means I want you to have the very finest and kindest thoughts about everybody and everything.

When happenings seem to trouble us, and make us feel sad and blue,
Someone is sure to show us inside, silver is shining through.
My little vase is in reverse, yet I think it very fine,
For it has a lining of deepest blue while outside the silver does shine.
I want to be like my silver vase; no matter how I feel
I want to be brave about it and only my smiles reveal.

LAUGHTER

Love,

Aunt Sadie

January 26, 1942

My dear little Anemone,

The name of the flower spray which I am enclosing is unknown to me, but I plucked it from a vase on my desk to send to you because it looked so pretty. I hope it will keep well enough until you get it, at least. Well, it seems that this is the last bit of stationery of its kind that I am now using to write to you. All the other pretty stationery is dwindling down very low. What do you suppose that means? Can it mean that I shall stop writing when I have no more? Oh, no! I shall continue to write. But it must mean that you will be coming home soon.

A Little While Longer
What is a little while longer when children are coming home?
We all grow a little bit stronger to know we are never alone.
Waiting, waiting a little while longer, time and space disappear,
And thus, our faith becomes much stronger, for those we love are ever near
Then we even gain the courage, perhaps to sing a little song,
Joyfully our hearts we nourish, to wait a little is not so long.

JOYFUL

    WAITING

        BRINGS

            VICTORY!

Aunt Sadie

January 27
1942

My dear little Persimmon,

Do you remember what I called you yesterday? I called you "Anemone," pronounced an-e-mo nee, and the second syllable gets the accent. The flower which I am sending you herein is an anemone. I also have a red one on my dresser. I had two purple ones, and that is why I chose it for you, so that we may each have one.

Your daddy called me up today, and told me some really wonderful things about you. I shall not be a bit surprised, one of these days, to hear that you are sitting up.

Anemone,
Someone I love has sent you to me,
How can I then fair words employ
To tell how deeply I enjoy, our petals o'erlapping,
Silky and rare, like the wings of a butterfly, delicate, fair,
Transparent as the light shines through.
Anemone, when I look at you,
I am glad, and my heart sings
For the beautiful thoughts your presence brings.

LOVE

Aunt Sadie

January 29
1942

To my dear little Cinnamon Bun,

Now, I have been a bad auntie again. I did not write to you yesterday. I will tell you why when I see you. If you ever miss a letter, be sure this is good reason why I did not write, but I think of you and love you all the time.

Your mother called me on Wednesday and told me a few things that made me very happy. I was glad to hear that it is pretty definite that you will be coming home in March. Of course, we do not know yet exactly what day it will be, but it sounds like soon. Then I was also glad to hear that your mother brought you a special kind of lipstick which cannot harm even children. I am sorry we did not think of it before, or else I would have it for you long ago. The third thing made me happiest of all, and that is that you are so good, and are continually happy and joyful. Be sure, my dear little Cinnamon Bun that is the best help to you of all.

Gracious, I wrote so much, there's no room for the poem, but don't be disappointed.

Here it is!

All night long the snow whirled 'round,
And noiselessly slept on the frozen ground;
I would use my new sled the next day!
Early next morn, the sun shone bright,
My dream, like the snow was no longer in sight,
For lo! It had melted away.

January 30, 1942

My dear little Cloverbloom,

> Music is playing in the room next door,
> Music I never heard before,
> And listening as I quietly lay,
> It seems to carry me far away.
> Now it tinkles gaily like bells in the snow,
> Now it rumbles rudely like thunder below,
> Then it sails as smoothly as a boat in the pond
> With waltz-tunes-a-gliding, of which I most am fond.
> Oh, I'll ne'er grow tired of my good neighbor's songs,
> For many happy hours, to them my thanks belong
> And best of all, I often find as I the rhythm keep,
> Before I know what I'm about I've fallen fast asleep!

Does that ever happen to you when you play the radio? I hear that Gloria is no longer near you, but the radio can be a very happy companion, too. Also, thoughts of me because I love you more each day.

BE EVER TRIUMPHANT

Aunt Sadie

February 1
1942

To my dear little Pussy-cat,

> *Early this morning, without any warning,*
> *On February one, a dear little bird, I suddenly heard, chirping in the sun.*
> *"What can this be?" Said I to me,*
> *"Old winter still is here"; said the birdie, land's sake,*
> *I make no mistake springtime is ever so near!*
> *I jumped out of bed, to the dear bird I said*
> *"Oh, thank you, my fine feathered friend."*
> *But the birdie took fright, and flew out of sight,*
> *And so the tale comes to an end.*

Well, your mother called me on Sunday, and congratulations, my dear, so you are promoted. Good for you!

It's just fine that you are coming home in March. Your mother and daddy spoke to the doctor and he said that you are getting along fine.

It was lucky that Uncle Ruby could come up to see you. I'll bet you were surprised! I also heard about the doll and the lovely painting set.

I was working on the poems for the book today. By that I mean I was thinking about it and talked it over with one of my friends. In about a week or two I shall really begin to prepare the manuscript. I shall always let you know how I am making out with it, whenever there is anything to say.

With carloads of hugs and kisses,

Aunt Sadie

February 2
1942

My dear little Chocolate Sundae,

Today was a very good day for me, and I'm sure you know the reason why. It was because of the lovely letter I received this morning from you. It was a real long one, too. I certainly want to congratulate you on being promoted, and on getting good marks, also. I know it is not easy to study when one is in bed, but the fact that you are doing it and doing it well, makes me very happy. It is quite all right that you are saving some books to read when you will be home, because then your mother may even want to read some of them with you. I know I shall certainly want to do so when I will visit you at home, and read aloud to you, and explain some parts as we go along.

> *Rippling clouds on a mid-winter night,*
> *Pale shines the frozen moon*
> *O'er the horizon she casts a cold light,*
> *While the North wind blows like a stormy typhoon.*
> *Harsh though the North wind be, and proud*
> *Now blowing near, now far,*
> *He has blown aside a ripply cloud,*
> *Revealing hidden sprinkles of star*

Love,

Aunt Sadie

February 4
1942

To my dear little General!

Attention, please!

What do you suppose? I thought I didn't have any more stationery like this left, but when I looked in my writing-paper box, I found this sheet with the soldier on it. Then I said to myself, "this is exactly what Rhoda needs today, in order to remind her that she is a soldier in case she has forgotten."

You see, Mother called me today and told me the good news that you have been promoted from the table to the floor! That is a very remarkable sign of your improvement. Do you remember that in the beginning of your exercises you were even afraid to be on the table, and now you are going to be courageous enough that you can take the more advanced exercises? That is truly wonderful! Do you know that if you think of me while you take your exercises you will improve even faster? And no harm whatsoever can really come to you. Try it next time.

Think of everybody who loves you. There are very many, are there not? You might try this too:

> *Once they had me on the table*
> *'Cause I wasn't very able to play upon the floor.*
> *Without the least bit fuss or trouble*
> *On the ground I now play water-bubble,*
> *And soon I shall do much more!*

ITS FUN TO BE BRAVE!—Aunt Sadie

FEBRUARY 8
1942

My dear little Chinnie-Winnie,

What are you doing today? This afternoon your mother called me up and made me very happy by telling me that you now roll over on your tummy when you take your exercise. That again is a very fine improvement, and if you want to make me much happier, do you know what you can do? Be braver than ever, and more heroic and trusting than ever before, and try out the exercises on the floor. Do you think you can do that for me very soon[?] And you shall see what a beautiful Valentine I shall send you!

Splashing in the water, swishing all around,
Friend water come to meet me from a hidden spring in the ground.
The sunshine is my brother, my sister is the air,
But water is a friend to all who welcome his kind care.

LOVE

Aunt Sadie

February 9
1942

To my dear little Apple-Turnover,

Today Uncle Morris called me up to ask about you, and of course it made him very glad to know that you are so much better and will be home soon. It is good you can "turn over."

Shall I tell you a secret? Well, don't be surprised if you get a Valentine from your cousin Donald too. I'm telling you you're certainly are a popular young lady! How do you do it? What is the secret of your charms, pray tell?

Today they turned the clock ahead
Though winter sleepy lies,
'Tis daylight when I go to bed and dark when I arise.

Are you getting used to the new hours? In my office we can't believe that it is time to go home at half past five because it is still so light.

When I take dictation and come to a pause,
I look out at the azure skies.
'Tis no fabrication, whatever the cause
I think of your deep blue eyes.

I do, too.

BEAUTY

Aunt Sadie

February 11
1942

Sweetie-Honey-Bunch,

Your mother called me and she said that you look "just wonderful." I am so glad to hear it. She also told me that you had some extra visitors. I hope you enjoyed their company.

Tonight, I am not going to write a poem, but I am going to tell you a little story.

Once upon a time I was afraid of the water. But I was so afraid, that I would even not dip my little toe in the ocean not even once in five years.

One day I went to the country. About a mile away there was a brook of running water. It was in a very beautiful spot, between two rows of mountain hills, and between these hills there were many bubbling waterfalls. The little waterfalls played and gurgled together on the rocks and formed the little brook.

The little brook was about five inches deep, and as you know, that is not deep at all. I had a great longing to go into that brook, wading. It was a very hot summer's day, and the water looked cool and inviting. My friends called to me. I had my swimming suit on, and suddenly I forgot about my fears because those who loved me were calling. So, into the brook I went.

Then the strangest thing happened. I sat down. Yes, just like that. And I felt the active little brook trickling and squirming where I sat, and on my heels and through my fingers. Then very gradually, slowly, slowly I rested on my elbows. I moved myself near to one of the tiny waterfalls, where the rock was a little higher, and let my shoulders rest on the rock-pillow. After that it was easy to let my head go, and feel the pleasant water playing around my neck and sliding through my hair.

Then came the biggest surprise of all. I was looking straight up at the bluest sky I had ever seen. And between me and the sky there was nothing, nothing except beautiful green lace, woven by the branches which met each other overhead as they grew from the trees standing on either side of the mountain-hills.

There I lay, as sweet and happy and contented as ever I could be. What did I think of? Why I thought of some poetry, something perhaps which I think you may even know. It goes like this:

> Great, wide, beautiful, wonderful world,
> With the wonderful water, round you curled,
> And the wonderful grass upon your breast,
> World, you are beautifully dressed.
> The wonderful air is over me,
> And the wonderful wind is shaking the tree
> It walks on the waters and whirls the mill,
> And talks to itself on the top of the hill
> World, you are so great, and I am so small,
> I tremble to think of you, world, at all,
> And yet, when I said my prayers today,
> A whisper within me seemed to say,
> "You are more than the earth though you are such a dot,
> You can love and think, but the earth cannot"

After that I was no longer afraid of the water. Now do you think that the next time you have to go in the pool, you will be able to look up at the ceiling and make believe you, too, are seeing such a beautiful world. For, after all, wherever we are, we can see a beautiful world.

Thousands of love and hugs and kisses,

Aunt Sadie

February 13
1942

My dear little Minnie-Ha-Ha,

So, the Hopi Indians paid you a visit! Now that is something! You must tell me more about it some day when I see you.

That was a sweet, sweet letter you wrote to me. Thank you. I received it when I came home tonight (Friday). Dear me, when I write on Fridays, I never know whether you will receive the letter on Saturday or Monday. Or do they deliver mail on Sunday also, where you are staying? Anyway, I am glad to learn that your schoolwork goes along well. But good gracious! What's the idea of having so many visitors on one day? Popular, eh? Well, as long as you had a good time, I'll forgive you. I'm sorry, darling but I may not be able to come up to see you for a couple of Sundays or so, but believe me, the moment it will be possible, I shall run to you.

Thanks for your greetings to my friends. It always makes them happy also, to hear from you. Did you have a happy St. Valentine's day? Can you guess which one was mine?

Love and kisses and a barrel of hugs,

Aunt Sadie

February 15
1942

My dear little Skylark,

Well, now, your mother called me today, and she told me all about the lovely Valentines you received. Good for you!

Your mother also gave me some good reports from a nurse with whom she spoke. You are going home sometime in March and shall probably be allowed to sit up for about five or ten minutes at a time. That is very, very good, as no doubt you can easily see.

I am not able to come next Sunday either, my dear, but if it will be possible, I shall run.

Graceful green leaves how proudly you stand, in a bed of water, lords of the land
Chinese water plant, year after year, you sprout fresh foliage contented to be here.
Neither fragrant nor colorful, as other flowers I know,
I can tell your character by the way you grow
Constant and strong, reared in simplicity,
Cheerful though meek, steeped in felicity.

STEADINESS

Aunt Sadie

February 16
1942

Dear, dear Daisy,

Can it be you are lazy or is it the sun in your eyes, that makes your heart glow so,
Your petals in white gleam so, and bid the fair maidens arise?
I'm not afraid when the room is dim, to open the door and to enter in,
For I know the darkness, (indeed I have no doubt),
Where to touch the switch that put the darkness out
When I get to be a grown up (as I'm sure I shall someday),
Perhaps I'll find another darkness, as I continue on my way
Nor shall I be a tremble, knowing well that I can win
All the Light in Heaven's Kingdom, if I'll only enter in.

Please excuse all my "crossings out," you know, if you write poetry you very often have to make changes. How is your smile today? I am looking forward to hearing some more good news about you on Wednesday.

SMILES

Love,

Aunt Sadie

February 19
1942

My dear little Lotus Blossom,

Have I ever told you what there is about you that I like best of all? No? Well, of course, it is hard to say, since there are many things about you which I like very much. Your hair and your eyes, and so on, are very sweet, to be sure, but the sort of things I like best are those which you cannot see, or touch but you <u>feel</u> them, and enjoy knowing it is in you. What do you suppose I mean? Well, for one thing, I mean a cheerful disposition, a kind and courteous manner, a loving heart. All these, you always do express, but the best of these is being thankful. I know that everything which you receive, makes you feel thankful, be it little or great. You are thankful for everything you can do, be it much or small. To have such a nature, such a quality, makes you the richest person in the world, and for this truth, you make me thankful too.

Let us join our thankful hearts, your heart and mine,
Other things may pass away, but the thankful are eternal as time.

ETERNAL

Love, hugs and kisses,

Aunt Sadie

February 21
1942

My dear little Joy bird,

Today is the day before George Washington's birthday, and we had a dance. I wore my evening gown to the dance in the evening, and I was in a minuet together with some other ladies and gentlemen. Someday I shall dance it with you. It is very simple and pretty. Then there was some funny entertainment about Jonah who was swallowed by a whale and lived for three days and three nights in the belly of the whale. It was a story from the Bible, but done in a very funny way, in a negro manner of speech, and we all laughed very much. In the minuet dance the gentlemen wore gray wigs as they used to do over a hundred and fifty years ago.

I've searched and searched for something to say,
Alas! I cannot find it, but I have a ball of yarn,
And I think I shall unwind it!

JOYFULLY

Aunt Sadie

February 22
1942

To my sweet little Lollypop,

Oh, I have so much to say, it will surely make up for two letters at least. First of all, since I've been a bad auntie again, my conscience has been bothering me, and I have been trying to excuse myself by saying something about mail deliveries, holidays, and so on.

Here it is:

> I send my letter through the mail,
> With perfect faith that it won't fail,
> To reach my loving little friend,
> Who awaits the message at the other end.

This morning, no, no, of course it was in the afternoon, your mother called and I was very happy to hear that your cold is all better, and that the doctor thinks you will probably be able to sit up by the end of March since you are doing so well with your massages and exercises.

After she called, I happened to be looking out of the window and I saw flocks of birds, (they looked like blackbirds or crows) flying northward. I said to my friend, Frances, "look its spring." Then she and another friend Rita, came and looked. They had never seen birds flying North or South before. Yes, they were flying to a colder climate because they must surely be feeling that the warmer weather is coming nearer to us.

> Blackbirds, blackbirds, northward flying
> Would make me laugh, had I been crying,
> But who can cry when I know they bring,
> Glad tidings of the coming spring.

So, little lollypop, together with me, let us look forward to a glorious

SPRING

Love,

Aunt Sadie (more mail tomorrow)

February 23
1942

My brave little Amazon,

I have bought a new book for you which I hope you will enjoy, in fact, I'm sure you will enjoy it. Your mother has it now and of course, she will save it for you. The name of it is "Pollyanna," the story of a little sweet girl who made other people happy by being just glad herself.

> *Freesias, freesias, shaped like a bell,*
> *Pretty you are, yet more sweetly you smell.*
> *A dot of pure gold rests in your center,*
> *Where all are enriched who dare to enter.*

Another poem:

> *A bottle of ink is a mystery*
> *For one can never tell what finally*
> *May flow from a pen inspired and free*
> *A story, a picture or just poetry.*

I hope you enjoyed your Washington's birthday holiday, no lessons. I am looking forward to hearing some more good news from mother on Wednesday as always.

MY BRAVE ONE

Aunt Sadie

February 24
1942

My dear little Mermaid,

Oh, how my heart thrills and jumps with happiness when I see a letter from you in my mailbox.

You say you will learn sometime how to spell the word "decimal." It is easy. D-e-c-i-m-a-l. That is all. It is not too difficult to learn decimals, in fact, it can even be very interesting.

About Sunday, it is practically impossible for me to come this Sunday. Perhaps I shall be able to make it the following week, or else maybe after that. Don't you worry at all if you lose any of my letters. I always copy the poems before I send you the letter. I only did not copy the first few poems I sent, and I know that your mother is saving these. I am glad to hear that you have new neighbors like Jean and her radio. Do you have fun often? Have all the fun and laughter you can get, provided of course, that you don't harm or disturb anybody else.

My friends are fine, thank you. Claire may go to Washington. She has been offered a better position there, and she may decide to accept it.

By the way, you forgot to put the return address on your letter, but as long as it was addressed properly to me, it arrived safely.

By the way again, you may have a surprise on Sunday. Your uncles are planning to visit you, Rubin and Harry, but don't set your heart on it, just in case, you know. So, continue to

BE GLAD

Aunt Sadie

February 25
1942

My dear little Choo-choo,

Your mother called me up again today (Wednesday), and told me all about the wonderful things Miss Baum is saying about you. And what shall I say? Only continue to improve as you have been improving. The best way to improve is by continuing to be cheerful and cooperative, and by thinking kindly thoughts of other people.

> *Red flowers with a yellow streak,*
> *Yellow flowers streaked with red,*
> *A moment ago, I heard them speak,*
> *And this is what they said:*
> *Child, you do not know my name,*
> *Yet you love me just the same,*
> *I love you too, oh little one,*
> *And bring you rays borne by the sun,*
> *Rays of light and joy and cheer,*
> *Welcome are both far and near,*
> *Though near or far, though one may ask,*
> *To spread the light, this is my task.*
> *Could I spread joy and cheer and light,*
> *As the red flowers I should be,*
> *And like the yellows too, I might*
> *Though none ask it of me.*

How is Miss Decimal today? Yes, it is becoming more definite that your Uncle Rubin and Harry are coming to see you on Sunday. Isn't it marvelous the way everybody loves you!

Love,

Hugs and kisses,

Aunt Sadie

February 26
1942

My dear little Tootsie-Wootsie,

> *A sunny afternoon, the side of a lake,*
> *I throw pebbles in as little pools they make*
> *Ripples spreading far to the side of the lake,*
> *On a sunny afternoon 'tis good to be awake.*
> *Though alive and awake, like the lake, I am calm,*
> *And events like the pebbles can do me no harm*
> *I am quiet, I am silent, drop the pebbles at will,*
> *Like the lake, in G-d's arms, I can be still.*

I have just written this poem about a picture which hangs on my wall. You may remember having seen it. It shows a pool on a sunny afternoon, with little shrubs growing around the edge, and underneath are written these words: <u>Be calm, Be quiet, Be silent, Be still</u>

So, I wrote about it in my way. Perhaps you can try writing sometime about something you have too, or something you see or think about. You know, I mean only if you feel like it.

No doubt you are anxious to begin reading some of the books you have at home. However, there is one book I should like you to read even before then, if possible. It is "Pollyanna." Please ask your mother to bring it for you. She has it.

No more until tomorrow, except a hundred hugs and kisses.

Aunt Sadie

March 1
1942

My dear little Succotash,

Shall I share a little secret surprise with you? Yes, indeedy! Here it is.

March 12th is your daddy's birthday, and of course I know you would like to give him a birthday present which would be a surprise. I have worked out a plan. I have seen some very special neckties which have been made by hand by the natives of the Netherlands East Indies. This is really something quite special, and I am going to buy one, something to go with your daddy's brown suit. Then sometime within the next few days, I will send it to you. You must keep it safely hidden until the 12th. Fortunately, March the 12th comes out on a Wednesday, when he may visit you, and of course you will give it to him. Perhaps I shall get a card for you to give to him also. Boy, oh boy, will he be surprised! Of course, he will wonder how you ever got it and you can have a lot of fun with that. How would you like that?

Meanwhile, I am happy to say that your mother called me up today and told me that you are looking lovely and are keeping very cheerful and enjoy the joke books. That is fine.

Welcome, welcome, month of March
I know it is needless to say
That true to tradition, you came in like a lamb
But how will you march away?

Love and hugs and kisses, kisses and hugs and love,

Aunt Sadie

March 2
1942

My dear little Sweetness-Neatness,

How is your smile today? Is it a great big one? Good for you.

This is really Christmas paper, but I hope you will excuse me for using it even if it is so near to Easter.

> *Pussy-willows in the Spring, thoughts of flight and fancy bring,*
> *Yellow jonquils in array, make indeed a festive day.*
> *I laugh, I play, I loudly sing, proclaiming "Hail it is the Spring"*
> *And though the blossoms bloom and burst, Spring*
> *won't be here 'till the twenty-first.*

Yes, my darling, eighteen more days until Spring will be here officially, although there are many signs in the air. I still haven't gotten a chance to get, you know what. I probably won't be able to get it until Saturday, but that's alright. The main thing is that I mustn't forget.

Your daddy called me up today. He tells me that Dr. Pistachio is going to examine you again soon. Did you know what? Well, Dr. Mulligan thinks you are just swell, and that makes me very happy.

I have to take my bath now, so I'll say good night, and I'll write again tomorrow.

Oodles of love,

Aunt Sadie

March 3
1942

My dear little Honeysuckle Lady,

Silver stars shine once again, brighter than before the rain,
They twinkle in the twilight air, happy to be stationed there.
In their place in the firmament, the silent stars are well content.
I, a little child, am here, loved, protected, free from fear,
Like the stars, I like to shine, knowing all I see is mine,
Mine to turn to joys and smiles, reaching, like the stars, for miles,
Again, like the stars, I sometimes blink, but here's the difference
I can think!

Of course, this poem was inspired by today's all-day rain. Better weather tomorrow, I hope.

How is Jean, who's next to you? Is she still there? Your mother tells me that you have some interesting parties with crackers and milk and so on. That is fine. Keep on enjoying yourself. I am looking forward to Wednesday afternoon when you mother usually gives me such good news. Remember, cooperation and cheerfulness are the way to your successes.

Give my best regards to your mother and to daddy (but don't tell him our secret yet).

Love and kisses,

Aunt Sadie

March 4
1942

My dear little Letter writer,

Whee! Did I have a grand good morning today when I found your very lovely letter in my mailbox!

Now about some of the news which you wrote. Don't you worry one bit about the secret. I will send it out in time for you to have it by next Tuesday or Wednesday, but not any sooner. So, you see there is really no problem at all, is there? That is how it is with very many things that happen to us. They seem tremendously difficult, but after we think it over, or talk it over, we find a solution (which means an answer).

My friends are fine, thank you, and I am very happy to see that Mrs. Morganstein thinks about you. Indeed, you must answer her very thankfully. Perhaps it can even be arranged that you may see her afterwards.

Now you are having long division by three numbers. That shows you are making progress. Of course, by putting in plenty of effort even this will become easy. Do you remember that at one time it was even difficult for you to divide by one number? But you will improve in the three-numbers division even as you did before.

Good for you that you will be sitting up soon. Needless to say, I am overjoyed to hear it. Your mother called me up today and told me how beautifully clean you looked. Beautiful thoughts always make us look clean.

May I make one or two suggestions to you? Yes? (otherwise) is written as one word, not as two words. Now separate the "nice" in half. What do you get? Ni-ce. Put an e in the middle ni e ce. That is how to spell my nice <u>niece</u>.

Love and kisses,

Aunt Sadie

March 5
1942

My dear little Honey-Lamb,

I still did not get <u>it</u>, you know what, but I shall get it on Friday or Saturday. This means you may expect a little package from me on Monday or Tuesday. Isn't that just grand?

People are rushing back and forth, to east, to west, to south, to north
But what their reason for rushing may be, is more by far than I can see.
They rush in the morning, at noon and at night,
When the stars are shining, and in broad daylight,
They come from the east, from the south, north or west
And I'm sure they don't know what it means to rest.
I wouldn't mind at all if their purpose were clear
If they hurried from January straight through the year
But I must confess, it makes no sense, to be very busy when it's all pretense
When I grow up, I dare to say, I shall live quite another way,
I shall make time to be gentle and mild
And to use my best manners, even to a child.

I didn't know this poem would turn out to be so long. Please excuse the lengthiness and also the crossing out-ness.

March 6
1942

To my dear little Cherry Chiffon Pie,

Um-um! Is that good!

Well, I had a different kind of surprise again today. Your daddy called me up and told me that he had telephoned Miss Baum, and that she said <u>some</u> wonderful things about you.

In the first place, it seems that Miss Baum likes you very, very much. Why do you suppose that is? I just wonder. Can it be because you are cranky? Oh, no, excuse me, it's because you are so smiley. But, what else did she say? That you will be sitting up very soon and of course, you know what that means. Safe home soon. Guess what! Tomorrow (that is Saturday), I am going to buy <u>it</u>. On Monday I shall send it out to you. Catch it.

What I say:

> *I sent a secret through the air*
> *I did not know that you might care*
> *But though it sped through many miles,*
> *I feel rewarded by your smiles.*

What you answer:

> *I did not know that I should care,*
> *To catch a secret through the air,*
> *But since it brought me many smiles,*
> *We can't be separated, even by miles.*

Tomorrow I shall be able to tell you more about my shopping expedition. I have to get some new writing paper too, because even after you will be home, I want to continue writing to you very often.

So, good bye for a day or two, and be well and happy.

Most lovingly,

Aunt Sadie

March 8
1942

My dear little Honey-Bell,

Now I can tell you about my shopping on Saturday. I got the necktie and I shall send it out on Monday. You will receive it on Tuesday, or early Wednesday, so you won't have to concern yourself about hiding it. I got some writing paper for you also which I hope you will be able to use. It has lines on the first page of each sheet, but not on the other three sections. You will see what I mean when you get it. I hope you will like it. The lines are in red and in blue and in the upper left hand corner there is a silly looking cow called "Bossy."

Your mother called me today, and as ever I was delighted to hear that you are getting better and better. It was too bad that I didn't know earlier that your daddy was going to look at a bungalow. Perhaps I could have made some arrangements to come. But this coming Sunday I shall do my very best to come without fail.

Buddy Bear looked all around as he bent his back and he stood his ground
He was plucking a flower, and it was plain to see,
that Buddy Bear was afraid of me
But I was afraid of little Buddy Bear
And so, I pretended that I didn't see him there
But my love for the flower was greater than my fears
So, I chased him away by boxing his ears.

Love,

Aunt Sadie

March 9
1942

To my dear little Poppy,

Today I mailed two packages for you. One package contains something for you, and the long one is for your daddy. The man in the post office said it would arrive there Tuesday morning. It if does, that will be just fine.

> Where does the soft cotton go to, in the early days of Spring?
> It's picked up by the birds as they twitter and chirp
> And carried off on their wing, then they drop it, ever so gently
> As hither and yon, they fly
> Then the delicate fluff forms into a puff
> Making boats that sail the blue sky.

This is a funny way of writing a letter. I started it at home last night. I wrote page one. This morning I wrote the poem, (page 2), in my office. Now, it is after lunch, and I am continuing. I shall have to hurry otherwise I'll be finishing somewhere in bed tonight, or at supper time.

Well, I merely want to add that I hope you will have a fine Birthday celebration on Wednesday for somebody's Thursday birthday. Frances (that's the girl with whom I live), had a birthday on Monday. We had supper with a few girls, and then we had a good time together. She had a birthday cake, too. Is Jean still near you?

Love and kisses,

Aunt Sadie

March 12
1942

My dear little Bon-Bon,

About two minutes after I mailed the postcard to you, your daddy called me up, and he told me all about the wonderful birthday celebration you made for him. How he liked your gift, and the children singing "Happy Birthday to You."

> When I go swinging 'neath the big oak tree,
> The little people come, and play with me
> There's a tiny elf with a red peaked cap
> He's feeling very frisky since his afternoon nap,
> While here on the swing, right below my very knees,
> The blue fairy floats just as gay as you please.
> Over here, over there, in the tall tufts of grass
> They dance with darting glance as they try to pass each other on the way
> Before the end of the day
> For when the daytime ends, and the sandman sends me to sleep
> In dreamland deep, my little people cry, as they bid me good bye,
> Then I kiss them good night, 'till the next morning light
> Finds me once more as the day before
> Swinging underneath the big oak tree
> With my dear little people surrounding me!

I made this one up from the picture which I am enclosing. Please save the picture, if possible, because I want to do something special about it.

I am hoping to see you soon, my darling.

Love and kisses,

Aunt Sadie

March 15
1942

My dear little Sweetness,

How can I express in words what I felt in my heart today when I called you at the hospital and your daddy told me the wonderful news that you have been sitting up since Saturday! And you were wearing a dress! We all know what that means. Home soon, very, very soon. Patience pays. And did your daddy tell you what I have been doing on Saturday and Sunday? I have been arranging all the poems to a book. There is a contest for a children's book which closes on March 31st. I am getting the book ready. Of course, it may not win the prize, but in that case the book will be in readiness to send to another publisher and then perhaps someone will like it enough to publish it. Everyone who reads your poems just loves them.

Claire and Frances are helping me to type them up and they certainly are enjoying the work. By the way, I found very attractive titles for them, and I am thinking of a good title for the entire group of poems. See if you can help me out. Whether it ever gets published or not, I want to make a special one for you, with pictures, and nicely bound. So, do you see what beautiful things you have been making possible? All because of your sweet, cheerful disposition.

I love you,

Aunt Sadie

P. S. Wish me luck

March 17
1942

My dear little Celebration,

Did you know that today is a holiday, St. Patrick's day, and the Irish people are celebrating by wearing green colored things because green is the color of their flag. There was a parade on Fifth Avenue, but I could see only a teeny-weeny part of it, because it was on my lunch hour and I had to go back to my office.

Do you know that I have not yet heard how you like the writing paper that I sent you, perhaps you don't like it at all.

Holiday Parade
I like to watch a parade, with colors flying and bugles crying,
And people marching division upon division
With rhythmic step and well-timed precision
I like to watch a parade
I like a holiday with a festive mood
Best, better or good are the clothes we wear
Leaving behind us all worry or care
I like a holiday

Another poem:

I have a new pink hat,
With a downy brown feather on top
And a brim that goes flippety flop
Hurrah for my new pink hat!

Love,

Aunt Sadie

March 18, 1942

My dear little Chrysanthemum,

Your mother called and I was very, very happy to hear that you continue to sit up with a back rest. That is really excellent. Now, the fact that you have to use the foot rest, or foot board, or whatever the thing is called, is no reason to make you enjoy the sitting up business any less. Do you understand what I mean? The foot board does not mean anything bad. It is merely a support for your footsies until they get stronger, just as the back rest is a support for your back. But the main thing is that you should use the best medicine, and of course you know what that is, miles of smiles, and also please remember the answer to the great riddle. What is the greatest thing in the world? LOVE. Then think of all the people who love you, and also think of all the people whom you love. That makes quite a few, does it not?

I saw
Cellophane spangles in purple and green,
In red, yellow pink and in brown
With pink eared bunnies, and chickies that scratch
With large speckled eggs in colors to match
Shouting, "Easter is coming to town"

Love and kisses

Aunt Sadie

March 19
1942

My dear little Scholar,

You made me very happy this morning by sharing your school marks with me. I think they are quite good especially the Spelling and the Penmanship. Indeed, I showed your letter to some girl in my office, (her name is Mollie) and we both agreed that your handwriting is better than the writing of some of the men who work there!

The arithmetic in 5B is not easy, so I think a mark of B is really good. Of course, when we are learning there is always room for improvement. As for the Geography, we will have a little conversation about it when you get home, and perhaps we can see what can be done. I remember I once talked to Rina* about her geography when she was a little girl, and I made some very interesting discoveries. After that, her marks in geography improved, and they were equally high as her other marks. I have a feeling that the same thing might work with us.

It is good you will be going home soon, and of course I know that a few days or less will not make too much difference to you now.

My friends are fine and are very glad to hear of your progress.

I have named all the poems in the book, and I have finished typing them. Now I have to find a title for the whole book and make an index.

Tons of love,

Aunt Sadie

---

* Rina was Sadie's niece and Rhoda's cousin.

March 20
1942

My dear little Honeydew,

Did you know that Saturday or Sunday is the beginning of Spring? Did Miss Aromstrom tell you? Spring is the time when everything returns to life again, all who live gain more strength and more aliveness, and the earth keeps nice and warm.

> One more day and spring will be here
> The earth will grow warm 'neath the touch of the sun
> The seeds in earth's bosom will awaken one by one
> And blossom and bloom in flower some cheer
> One more day and I shall rise
> To greet the warm sun as it kisses my cheek
> And the breeze through my hair as it plays Hide-and-Seek
> While my praises of nature ascend to the skies.

Please excuse me for running out of ink, and having to use pencil, but at the moment as I am writing I am not in a place where I can get some ink so I continue this way. As I wrote you before, all our poems are typed and they all have very attractive titles. I also have some sub-divisions in the book and here are some of the titles:

"Nonsense and Knick-Knacks," "Wonderful World,' "Ships a-Sailing," "Enter in"

How do you like these? I expect to have a busy weekend putting the finishing touches to our book.

Be Happy!

Lovingly,

Aunt Sadie

March 23
1942

My dear little Honey-Bunny,

Did you know that after I visited you, I was singing and laughing all the rest of the day? Do you know why? It was because I found you so much improved, and also, because of your wonderfully cheerful spirit. After your daddy came down, he spoke to Doctor Mulligan, and although we still do not know a definite date, the doctor said that it would be about a week after Easter, or so. Well, here's hoping! He also said that it would be a few days or so after you have been on the chair, but of course how soon <u>that</u> will be, is still a mystery.

When the proper time comes, I believe Miss Aromstrom will take the necessary steps to see that arrangements are made for you to have a teacher come to you at home. Isn't that also very good?

I really wanted to answer the question you asked me, but there was little time to do so. I will try to explain to you now. I am referring to your question about the poems, how did you help me to write them? Well, you see, I thought about you, first of all, and then I thought how nice it would be if you could hear from somebody you know and loved, every day. Then it might not seem so long between visits. Then, of course, there was the problem of what to write about. You can't just say, "I'm fine, how are you?" every day! Therefore, I had to look around for topics.

Now I believe that something beautiful and worthwhile can come out of the most ordinary article, if we only have the right thoughts about it. So, I had to have the good thoughts, and you must know by now that good thoughts bring the correct words. That is how I happened to write about such things as a lamp, or a rocking chair, or a hat. Then you also inspired me by your sweetness, and kindness and cheerfulness and thoughtfulness.

That is how you helped me write the poems. That is why I call them <u>our</u> poems. Now do you understand?

Love,

Aunt Sadie

March 24
1942

My dear little Lilac Bunch,

I was still thinking about Sunday and the wonderful time I had with you. Well, I guess the next time I'll see you will be the day when you come home. I know some new desserts. You must remind me to tell your mother about them so that she can make them for you.

> *Cutlets and omelets, pancakes and pies,*
> *Cornflakes and milkshakes, and bread made of rye*
> *Salads, raw carrots with creamed tuna fish*
> *Each of these makes a delectable dish*
> *All kinds of fruit with ice cream to boot*
> *Raspberries, strawberries very well suit*
> *To make the mouth water of my mother's daughter*
> *Knowing that she is preparing for me*
> *Muffins and puddings and southern corn pone*
> *To eat when they greet and welcome me home*

I'm sure you would have a very fine tummy ache if all those things were mixed in together. Of course, being wise you will indulge one at a time.

I still have not sent our poems away because one of my friends is reading them first and she has not yet returned them to me.

Claire and all those who know about you, were very happy that you are making such fine progress, and that you remember to think about them. Keep up the good work, my dear.

Love,

Aunt Sadie

March 25
1942

My dear little Fezziwig,

How are you today? But of course, I know all about it. Your mother called me today and told me that Miss Baum said you showed very good improvement since the last month, according to the test which she gave you. Isn't it simply marvelous the way the hospital care and treatment is helping you. Then in another couple of weeks or so when you get home, you will get additional things which will help you to grow better and stronger, such as you don't get there. For example, you will be out just in time for the nicer warmer weather and get the sun directly, especially when you will go to the country. Then also, there will be new things to eat and so on but, I better not tell you. I only meant to remind you that even though there are many good points now there will be still more later on.

Do you want to hear something funny? When I asked Larry what he wants me to bring him, do you know what he says? "Buy me a bat!" Can you imagine him with a bat? I can't.

By the way, I think your hair is getting nicer and nicer. Does that girl ever fix it for you during the week, or is it special only for visitors?

Love,

Aunt Sadie

P. S. I still have not sent our book away. I will let you know the minute I do. But meanwhile,

JUST BE GLAD

March 27
1942

My dear little Sweetness,

Could you ever imagine little pussies and huge, big dragons living together in perfect harmony and beauty? I never could, but when I came home from my office last night, that is what I found. There in a great white vase were, no, no of course not <u>real</u> pussies and dragons, but nice fuzzy, wuzzy, Pussy-willows in their gray furry coats and delicate yellow Snapdragon flowers, mostly in buds.

> I'm not afraid of dragons when they're standing in a jar
> They have changed their very nature and now snapdragons they are
> Nor do I fear the pussies which with the dragons stand
> For they neither purr nor spit when I stroke them with my hand
> If all the beasts upon this earth would change for the better
> And a better world it would be

I got the book of poems back only yesterday, from my friend and so I still have not sent them away. But tomorrow I am quite sure I shall send our book away. I will let you know. I am looking forward to Sunday to hear some more good news about you.

Does Angie still fix your hair, and has Jean gone home yet?

Well, I guess I shall say goodbye until tomorrow or so, and by the way I am thinking about vacation weekends with you, at least once in a while.

Remember just be glad.

Love,

Aunt Sadie

March 29
1942

Dear little Pussywillow,

Today is Sunday, but first I must tell you about Saturday. I took our book of poems up to the office where the contest is being held and when I handed it to the lady at the desk, she caught her breath and she said, "Oh, how beautiful it looks." So that was good wasn't it?

Then I saw your daddy for lunch, and we talked about your going to the country. Won't that be wonderful? Today your mother called, in fact, only a few minutes ago. She told me that you are very cheerful, and that you are now able to sit up with the backrest, but that you do not do so because you know that you must not. I was very glad to hear that Miss Baum found a good improvement in your last test, too. That is marvelous.

I am enclosing a little twig from the pussy-willows which I have in my white vase. When you come home, I shall get you plenty of flowers. There is a very nice florist near these rooms not like in the other place where you had to look for a mile before you could find one.

So long, until tomorrow and good, good luck.

Love and hugs and kisses, and don't forget, I'm going to collect them all when you come home.

Aunt Sadie

March 31
1942

My dear little Jonquil,

How are you feeling today? As you know Easter is but a few days away, and anything at all is liable to have happen on Easter. Bunnies come with the most precious gifts, and leave them here and there in a most mysterious way. So, if the funny bunny comes to leave something with you don't be too much surprised.

Tulips are growing in my garden
In purple, and yellow, pink, red and white
Exquisite they all are in beauty, tremendous some are in height
We, too, grow in the garden of G-d, beautiful souls have we all
And each is tremendous in something, be young or old, big or small
In what would you be tremendous, in size or in mind or in grace?
If 'tis character strength you would grow into there matters not station or place

Tomorrow is April Fool's Day, so have a good time and don't let too many people fool you. Think up a good one for your mother, but don't scare her.

I am writing this letter the very first thing Tuesday morning and I am <u>hoping</u> to write you another tonight, if all is well.

Love, hugs and kisses

Aunt Sadie

ABOUT SHARI LYN ANDERSON

Born in Brooklyn, New York and raised in Chestnut Ridge New York, Shari's life's journey brought her family to Portland, Oregon, where she's lived for the past 30 years. Shari immersed herself in the Jewish community and got involved in Leadership programs and volunteer work shortly after moving here. Over the years, she received awards and recognition for her involvement from the Jewish Community. Since retiring and caring for her mother, Shari had the opportunity to start a project that touched her heart. She had always dreamed about writing a book, though this is not the direction she thought it would take her, but she was overjoyed that she was directed on this path. Shari is looking forward to more writing adventures!

To comment or hear more about future books
join Aunt Sadies Letters on FB.

Aunt Sadie and Rhoda

CPSIA information can be obtained
at www.ICGtesting.com
Printed in the USA
JSHW030045150722
28124JS00006B/13